Integrated Delivery

Integrated Delivery

Innovating Leadership for Outstanding Healthcare Outcomes

David Stehlik, DSL

BEP

BUSINESS EXPERT PRESS

Leader in applied, concise business books

Integrated Delivery: Innovating Leadership for Outstanding Healthcare Outcomes

Copyright © Business Expert Press, LLC, 2021.

Cover design by Charlene Kronstedt

Interior design by Exeter Premedia Services Private Ltd., Chennai, India

First published in 2021 by
Business Expert Press, LLC
222 East 46th Street, New York, NY 10017
www.businessexpertpress.com

ISBN-13: 978-1-95334-956-9 (paperback)
ISBN-13: 978-1-95334-957-6 (e-book)

Business Expert Press Healthcare Management Collection

Collection ISSN: 2333-8601 (print)
Collection ISSN: 2333-861X (electronic)

First edition: 2021

10 9 8 7 6 5 4 3 2 1

Description

The 2020 pandemic proved past best practices too brittle for future challenges. An integrative model of leadership, synergizing the competing values and approaches of other models, is needed. This book focuses on the innovative leadership framework that can support emerging best practices in health care organizations. The practices of innovation and strategic management are indispensable.

Within, you will read about:

- Health care's past, present, and future trajectory,
- How innovation is related and required for ongoing success (and the different kinds of innovation at a leader's disposal), and
- The components and practices of strategic management, and how they integrate into the three modes of leadership: anticipatory, strategic, and administrative. Each is highlighted and the attributes of supporting tools summarized.

Unlike other leadership books, this one offers a systemic and sustainable perspective. This approach is not simply a "sustain the moment and worry about tomorrow later" approach. It is a "sustain the future, integrating it into our present paradigm now" approach. Especially important is the effort taken to explain and apply matters related to uncertainty, anticipation, as well as approaching future readiness.

Keywords

leadership; healthcare; management; strategy; innovation; strategic planning; effectiveness; technology; administration; foresight; integrated delivery; efficiency

Contents

Preface

When Your Best Is Contextual

During the NBA Playoffs of 1988, 1989, and 1990, internationally recognized super athlete Michael Jordan faced a crippling opponent in the Detroit Pistons and suffered sequential defeats. The Pistons were unified in subduing Jordan's scoring prowess and used physical and psychological leverage to bind him. With Jordan restrained, the Bulls had little recourse to hinder the Pistons' operation. At the time, Jordan's game had not matured enough to exploit the weaknesses in the Pistons' strategy; instead, he only saw the threat their teamwork posed to his talent; and, he was not one easily given to change. He was the prodigy and this was his domain. One can only imagine how different those three years of "almost" reaching the finals might have concluded had Jordan grasped the opportunity available and changed his strategic paradigm rather than sticking in his heels to prove his greatness—only to fall short each time, suffering the Pistons' mockery.

As with Jordan's predicament, success is not simply a matter of applying more strength to the current lever. Sometimes, success means knowing to change the focal point and leveraging your strength differently. This is the proverbial story of spinning your wheels, a situation where revving your vehicle's RPMs does little more than flick and spit mud, sand, and snow rather than offer the needed grip to propel your vehicle forward out of the unintended and discouraging predicament. Most have faced this kind of crisis in both personal and corporate life, and if not, one should count himself fortunate (while also preparing his mind for when it happens). And, this is ultimately about that. Hopefully not, but you might be thinking what this anecdote about NBA gamesmanship has to do with excellent administrative leadership in health care organizations, and the answer is in the principle: your singular strength is not enough. The recipe for excellence is far more complex than a one-person show, and if we forget to approach our organizations with that understanding, then we will likely fare as Jordan did, running into traffic every which way we turn, confused as to why our efforts are stilted and our teammates seemingly uninvolved and checking out. Alternatively, there are other lessons we can learn. From the Pistons we can see that great strategies provide psychological confidence and motivate action. Even individuals not prone to lend a hand get involved if the purpose behind the task supersedes their momentary interest. Additionally, the right execution of an appropriate strategy can nullify stronger competitors. Without direction, talent and potential overpromise. Even innovative organizations are susceptible to industry defeat at the hands of more consistent performers. Why? Outcomes trump creativity. That reality is why change management operations are difficult to execute, because we understand the present and know what works—even if much does not.

Change Begets Change: For Better or Worse

It goes without saying that health care is changing the world over. If nothing else, the global pandemic of 2020 highlights this reality. What is driving this change? While technology is a driver, the matter is far larger than simply computers and scanned documents or mobile measuring devices and iPhones. Social philosophies are changing—physicians are not "all-knowing" anymore, as what we think we need to know can be found online. Political involvement and governance considerations play larger roles in determining "what's safe." Moreover, one cannot ignore the economic weight of the sector, once measuring a full fifth of GDP, and soon far more once the pandemic expenditures are calculated. Truly, healthcare—specifically in the United States—is changing more from the merging streams of various domain changes (global shifts), and these changes are of differing strengths and speeds. Thus, to identify and propose a solution as being systemic while at the same time focusing solely on the repercussions experienced within a single driver's domain (like technology, energy, or population), is to offer well-intended medicine without accessing the patient's history of allergic reactions to the medicine's ingredients. To offer half-baked solutions will not help, and could even exacerbate current circumstances, and so I attempt to offer a chance at glimpsing the full picture, from the sector's past to its present, encouraging the application of the best tools for the future's sake.

In the chapters that follow, you will be introduced to a framework that integrates the best business and social dynamics concepts, strategies, and practices to healthcare. Health care has a tricky past. As much as we may want to think the past was golden in some manner or less difficult to manage—and that we should return to it—the reality we face is that such desires offer no aid in changing the present except to add discontent to our mounting concerns. Understanding how the old emerged into the new, this behemoth of a social and institutional structure, will act as an important first step as to understanding why health care thinking today is both more flexible than the markets in some areas and less in others. Next, you will discover how transformational changes in technology were nurtured through leadership practices that are often valued in isolation without a unified framework to join them properly. Ultimately, the core issue is only more aggressively highlighted by:

- The shifts in the business of health care;
- The academics and training for health care;
- The politics of health care; and
- The social implications of health care.

Certainly, you realize like most good practitioners that not everything needs reforming, and those things which do, do not all need reforming within the same window of time. Along the same lines, many calls for change within the sector have come and gone without the change ever taking place or sticking around. In that regard, the ideas in this book should be a welcome addition to keep the fire burning and motivate the troops who are already singing the anthem.

So What's the Prize?

If you are a leader in any organization or industry, then this book can help you, but if you are a health care leader, then I sincerely believe not reading this book might actually hurt you. Why? The systems approach to leadership outlined (Chapter 4) and detailed within (Chapters 5–7) will force a qualitative change in how you think about leadership, who you think of as a leader, and what you do as a leader. That last part is critical, because as we are all aware: it is not what you know, but what you do, that matters. Leadership leaves evidence. Health care is ripe with opportunity for the integrative leadership model's approach (advocated within) to evolve our organizations into high-performance, innovative pillars of the social fabric that can once again capture the American heart for their excellence, attentiveness, and prospection. Rarely does an industry touch people as often, as deeply, and as seriously as ours. Rarely is there a favorable moment such as now, when the gap (potential) and execution capacity exist alongside the available resources to bridge it.

This book explains how leadership practices are not all created equal. They are built on assumptions that have presumptive power during different points in the organization's lifecycle. Having this book, you have the opportunity to understand why your organization functions or dysfunctions in the present according to your leadership practices. Moreover, you can use this book as a guide to overcome dysfunction and exceed present success in the future with organizational change efforts according to a needs-appropriate level and operational purpose.

Prior to my detailing of the integrative leadership model, you will find out how health care has changed over the decades (Chapter 1), what innovation really means (Chapter 2), and how to think clearly about strategic management and its constituent parts of strategic thinking, strategy development, and strategic planning (Chapter 3). Then, I discuss the other models that contributed conceptually to the development of the integrative leadership model along with a description of the model itself (Chapter 4). The next chapters (Chapters 5–7) explore each of the three modes of leadership practices (anticipatory, strategic, and administrative) that keep an organization focused and refreshed throughout its various innovation-minded, effectiveness-establishing, and efficiency-building pursuits. After finishing, you will have a clear grasp of the model, but you may still wonder about integrating the model into your own leadership habits (or scaling it for the organization). To this end, I provide a short story (Chapter 8) about a health care organization in which the model is not spoken of, though its existence is clearly perceived. The imaginary organization illustrates ways in which the theory that undergirds the model and the practices that bring it to life can have a home in your organization.

This book is not a call to take it easy. Health care needs more than that. This book then is not leisure reading. Imagine it as an adventure manual, an open mission. Adventures are the transformative experiences that challenge us mentally, physically, and emotionally. Invite others to read it and work through it with you, implementing the good ideas and practices you draw out. You now have my map and descriptions and recommendations for your journey. The question before you is not whether the change I argue for is possible. It is. Others have proven it. The question before you is whether you really *want* this kind of change. Your time is too valuable to read without the purpose to implement. Make this experience purposeful and give it your all.

Godspeed,
David Stehlik, DSL

Introduction

Note: This introduction hosts the ideas and concepts which lay the foundation for the rest of the book. Thus, in the way the correct words are necessary for meaningful sentence writing but insufficient substitutes for explaining the sentence's full meaning, so also is this introduction an insufficient substitute for the meaning made by the chapters that follow. It is not the book, but it will ensure you can read the "sentence" that is the rest of the book most clearly.

The Remaining Constraints of the Past and the Future's Uncertainty

If your journey through the health care forest has been as multidirectional as most, then you understand the internal and external challenges of "proving" that your breadth of learning (as much as your depth) is of great value to a highly focused practice facing varied difficulties when urging organizational change. Successful, sustainable change requires the agreement and unified efforts of a multitude of people, and leaders are viewed responsible for more than just their own effort. That accountability is what good leadership expresses. At the same time, if clients, peers, bosses, or subordinates honestly knew how leaders felt going into every project, then they might add more fuel to doubters' fires, and few efforts would get off the ground.

At the same time, health care itself is a very nebulous field, where many seemingly unrelated factors are in play and issues at stake. For that reason, many leaders have added trouble in navigating the industry. There is no recognized guiding framework for what to learn and keep apprised of, causing many to feel lost in halls without knowing where to go or who to ask for help. That is where this book comes into play: by providing a framework for understanding how to build bridges through the uncertain waters of the present with innovation as your construction material and a portfolio of leadership practices as your building process. Instability and uncertainty are the name of the leadership game, and it would be rare to find a leader who disagrees. *Leadership in this environment, then, no longer draws on the imagery of rocks and mountains and internal stability, but instead calls forth notions of flow and signaling. The former concepts were key to promoting leadership integrity and sticking with internal plans until their fruition. The latter, however, urges smooth operations under environmental constraints as well as the recognition and flexibility to adapt given external shifts.* To illustrate the issue, consider that a self-aware man can still be run over by an oncoming semi if *all* that he is aware of is himself.

Balancing Perspectives: Right Priority, Right Time

To better understand the need for the kind of full-orbed leadership required by modern organizations, consider the story of Intel's leadership during its founding and early decades (located after this chapter's summary: Leadership "Intel" Snapshot). Intel's leadership team embodied Peter Drucker's three facets to the ideal executive, one (in this case, a leadership team) who is both externally and internally facing (recognizing how the markets affect us and recognizing how we organize and operate) while also active (how we change). Intel's leadership promoted a uniquely empowered organizational culture and adapted to answering the right questions the organization faced at the right times. The makeup of Drucker's ideal executive is a hearty rebuke to most industries' leaders and strategy models (competition, resources, or execution-focused). How many of us truly hold those perspectives in right balance (not meaning equally) on an ongoing basis? Those in health care face an incredibly insular environment, where clinicians are laser-guided to address acute issues that need immediate solutions. Thus, perhaps two of the three ideal executive facets might be well managed, and the executive team might make up for the third through nonclinical administrators, but tension remains that might be wrongfully blamed on the practice or nonpractice of medicine. The real issue, however, has entirely to do with the temporal perspectives in opposition (present vs. future).

The Intel example makes us aware that organizational success requires apparently paradoxical perspectives to be present and at play within the leadership function. Leadership teams need to have a diversity of priorities, across multiple time scales, at varying magnitudes in their decision matrix. Furthermore, Intel has succeeded in market relevancy for decades when others rose and perished. What kept them innovative at the *right* moment has to do with their approach to organizational decision making and leadership practices tied to organizational maturity.

Before addressing innovation, and its role in the future of outstanding health care outcomes, it makes sense to make a few points about the world we are not living in: the world we grew up in. We were raised in a world that no longer exists, by individuals who were also raised in a world that had long perished by the time they raised us. However, that did not stop them from raising us according to the norms of the former world, as if its character universally applied to our circumstances and would affect us similarly, giving us similar or equal advantages and constraints.

This is not a discussion of mores and values; instead, it is a point about how change ought to matter to our perspective. A healthy view of change—macro, meso, and micro, across varied categories—illustrates that prior generations' expectations are no longer adequate in providing frameworks for understanding phenomena and responding adequately. We need frameworks for recognizing change at different levels and then integrating decisions that consistently acknowledge those multilevel changes.

Society has changed and we can no longer respond within it as we used to. Our old paradigms no longer deliver as promised. Notice, I did not say we can no longer hold the same values or respond to change with former paradigms in an absolute sense. What is said is that we cannot expect the same results from our responses. In a phrase, the rules of the game have changed, and the old strategies no longer play as well as they used to. What tools and mindsets has it taken for *you* to succeed? Would the same adequately prepare today's new leaders in health care? How about those engaged in banking, or software development? Are they entering the computer age of the 1980s, 1990s, or early 2000s? Would any of us suggest that yesterday's equipment stands up to the rigor or the rules of today's arenas? Again, that does not mean the tools of yesterday are absolutely inadequate in all situations; rather, it means they cannot be *assumed* adequate for all present scenarios seemingly analogous to circumstances from the past. New insights for the sake of contemporary application are necessary to ensure the tools' continued value.

You Don't Know What

Let's review the basic supply and demand diagram. These are the quick chalkboard/whiteboard graphs that identify intersections of price (y-axis) and quantity (x-axis) for particular goods and services, having one line slanted downward from the left to the right (demand) and one line slanted upward from left to right (supply) (see Figure I.1).

Essentially, the former identified the prices at which a person would be willing to purchase one additional unit (assuming they began somewhere on that line, the "schedule"). For the latter, it identified the price at which a person would be willing to sell one additional unit (again, assuming they began somewhere on the schedule).

Old paradigms constrain you to seeing the environment in a partial way. This further constrains your capacity for responding to the environment. Modern businesses act a lot like this in their approach to price setting. In health care, we have schedules and negotiated rates as well. Certainly, there are multiple payment constructs, of which some, like prospective payment, might still attempt to fit into the supply and demand curve paradigm. Though we may not have realized it at the time, those interesting little graphs constrained our thinking. They forced us

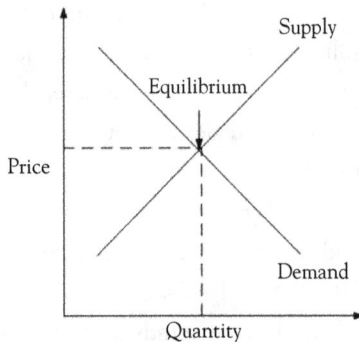

Figure I.1 Supply and demand curve diagram

into thinking we could have precise measures of aggregate demand in our markets as well as aggregate supply and know where we currently fit.

Given the increasing complexity of modern markets for all kinds of goods, services, and ideas, resulting from the increasing number of players, regulations, networking, and opportunities, it is increasing difficult to gain even a semblance of complete knowledge over our markets. Remember, complete knowledge is what we need for more accurate forecasting and decision making according to old models. From this, we can say that data mining for capitation estimates is an example of technology-supported inquiry racing against data complexity. Our paradigm is worse off now than when we first begun.

To grasp our dilemma, we need a better paradigm for dealing with uncertainty. The difference lay between the concepts of search and discovery. The former, search, entails a perspective assuming information you need is available, collated, and ready for processing. That being established, once they've located the data point in question, the leader might get to the real work of production/service delivery at the levels their market is primed for, at that price their market's payers will bear (or negotiate or force). The latter paradigm assumes information is knit together like a quilt by those who scavenge for associable components. It assumes the market served, the collaboration or lack thereof faced, the manner of service, they are all data points on a graph of unknown size with unknown scale, that is, without a coordinating framework. In this view, we, the "entrepreneurs," meaning individuals attempting to coordinate the market, give meaning to the data points themselves. We supply the context by coordinating information sharing (such as agreeing freely on prices) and thereby coordinate market transactions so that value previously locked can be freed.

In real life, the difference is that the former view propagates gathered information as being fixed into the present framework; so, for instance, an insurer's unwillingness to pay a particular rate elicits a response from us that such is normal, given past experiences in such negotiations. The explanation for behavior is already in the system. From the latter perspective, we would process the information differently. We would not automatically assume the reasoning and causal links. In fact, it may help us form a new hypothesis about how our market acts and how we should adapt to it or try to influence its ongoing evolution.

Let me note a few more points about this economic concept recognized as the knowledge problem (incomplete information)[1] before advancing. This concept provides a basis for understanding systemic uncertainty. In a sense, this book showcases a model for successful leadership amidst systemic uncertainty. We have to overcome major issues to improve our health care organizations and/or systems, and understanding those issues better should help us in the process of identifying and employing better solutions. *If our solutions do some nice things but do not truly address the problems we set out to conquer, then we will still lack the outcomes we intended.* That lack of focus will not serve our patients and stakeholders well. Thus, the knowledge problem matters to us because it pertains to the training, preparation, and dissemination of information that leads to systemic understanding—from the entire industry to single patients. That is, all of these efforts are incomplete. However, our approach need not be deficient if we can stop defining success on the completion of our information and instead measure it according to our speed to effective, rightly ordered responses.

The question here is: Who knows enough to make the best decisions in a given context? Is it feasible that one expert person gather, process, and execute upon all necessary information for an economy to smoothly and profitably operate? Those with an unfavorable impression of centralized planning operations would answer negatively, pointing out that decision making yields the most favorable results for decision makers rather than those directly affected by the decisions. You cannot value scarce goods and services properly in accord with market demand without subjective valuation playing its role, empowering indulgence and abstinence to the measure that each deems "enough."

Before it seems we are straying too far afield, imagine how this knowledge problem relates to the early discussion of how the world is changing. Imagine how incomplete knowledge relates to the kind of education those entering your industry are receiving. Who is setting that agenda? Are new

---

[1] Kirzner, I.M. 1973. *Competition and Entrepreneurship.* Chicago: The University of Chicago Press.

recruits entering with the knowledge requisite for success—success today or success a decade prior? Might we argue the internship industry has blossomed in part for this reason, that higher education has had difficulty adjusting to the rapidity of complex change for the environments and practices they are supposed to be preparing the next generation for? If so, should we expect such educational environments, unless they transform to offset this weakness, to be adequate preparatory systems? Is this not a reason for why clinical-type experiences are so crucial to preparedness?

So, to bring us back to why the notion of incomplete knowledge matters for us, remember that incomplete knowledge is a reality that is exacerbated as social change speeds up. Search paradigms increasingly fail. Discovery paradigms increasingly succeed (in their assumptions of capability). Thus, if incomplete knowledge used to be less of a hindrance to top-down, centralized planning processes, it becomes an even more powerful deterrent of success (read: well-coordinated exchange, or value creation) when more data points are generated from discovery and the possibilities for change increase.

Brought down to the individual level, the question of incomplete knowledge and search vs. discovery paradigms brings out the difference between thinking powerfully and thinking well. Thinking powerfully aligns with the notion of search, with the idea that you can parse through available information and select the best option. To think well, however, means understanding that all possible choices are not yet contained within your purview. There may be a better choice beyond the searchable set. Or, there may be no good choice at all. Thinking well expands the boundary of choices (direction and dimension of available options) and allows for the emergence of assumptions to the degree they may even replace old ones or combine with them. It manifests understanding. Truly, we need both kinds of thinking as leaders. Thinking well is akin to the pursuit of right understanding, and thinking powerfully facilitates action. Both are required for us to gain and employ wisdom. Furthermore, this discussion bears weight in matters of creativity and imagination. For instance, in higher education, the power of thinking might be demonstrated through the process of solving problems according to defined rules and prevailing assumptions, while the wellness of thinking might be demonstrated in the approach one takes to an unprecedented research project, instructing as to what resources may prove valuable or even that such resources could exist. The former relates to operating within a structure, leveraging strategic strengths at the right times and places in order to yield an expected result as quickly, cheaply, or with as much quality (or combination thereof) as possible. The latter relates to creating a structure for conveying thought.

Consider the rare, revolutionary shifts in thinking which occur in given fields of scientific study and practice.[2] They may or may not happen suddenly, and our modern way of life is dependent on the gains they promote. But, once they come into existence—you may have guessed it—they transform into a structure for powerful thinking. Thus, the pattern is thinking well (which entails thinking differently) precedes thinking powerfully; but, it is far more difficult to think well in a manner that results in a paradigm surpassing the one presently dominating. For that reason, we tend to find it more profitable to improve our power of thinking than to hope our wellness of thinking will lead to a different structure superseding the dominant paradigms.

Furthermore, suspending the dominant paradigm is difficult because it constantly argues for its own "logic" in our hypotheses, discussions, practices, and conclusions. In clinical practice, the prescription can only emerge from what is already known. That is the power of diagnosis. Conjecture's rightful place is elsewhere. In management practices, which are addressed in later chapters, thinking powerfully predominates intentions. This is why steadily increasing output and efficiency are usually its twin hallmarks. The notion of doing something else, however, is a hallmark of thinking well, the choice to operate under new assumptions (or a combination of new and old) in order to produce far better results (or even count results differently). If the driving assumption is that results will be marginally better, then approaching the matter with powerful thinking is more reasonable (since the aim in both is producing a kind of "good" thing), that is, it takes fewer resources to operate according to what already exists than to have to first successfully develop a new operating structure.

In some measure, this is also a discussion for product, business model, and market innovation. We have already brought up the matter of higher

---

[2] Kuhn, T.S. 1970. *The Structure of Scientific Revolutions*, 2nd ed. Chicago: The University of Chicago Press, 1970.

education, and it is evident the industry's delivery model is shifting toward less resource-intensive systems. Nearly the same methods of instruction are employed, but the information itself is nearly unlimitedly accessible whereas it was formerly constrained as a scarce resource. For the medical field, the question of education may soon face similar release—especially with the advancement of virtual and tactile interaction technologies. Of course, credentialing remains a pivotal barrier to entry. The same goes for many other professional designations where the information is freely available but practice authority remains in the hand of some accrediting body (CPA, PMP, CFP, etc.). Again, this brings forth the question we all must deal with inside and beyond our organizations:

- Should resources be spent to protect the prevailing structure, project, vision, or paradigm; or, should resources be spent to transform them?
- Which should we do personally, as leaders, within our organizations as we face opposition?
- Which should our organization do if and when we perceive regulatory threats to new practices, technologies, or policies that could strengthen our market share because we serve our patients/clients better?

We will face competitors who, if they cannot compete on product and/or service, and if they have no desire for collaboration, will seek to oppose us through powers separate from the service provided to our patients/client. We cannot be blind to the use of political leverage to suppress transformation, whether inside of our organizations or beyond them. Sometimes, our teams have seen more leaders rotate through leadership positions than they care to count, and so their unwillingness to trust the next leader is less a function of disloyalty and more of a function of prizing the stability of what has proven true and useful in all their years of service. Additionally, capital-intensive projects that have failed or did not live up to their hype in the past produce corporate memories we are held in comparison to—regardless of whether that seems fair. The same wariness can and does exist among stakeholders who may be encouraged or discouraged through political action, which market opponents support. In fact, getting in front of such issues is a topic for discussion in later chapters. That all being said, this notion of expanding options (discovery; thinking well) and choosing among them (search; thinking powerfully) for the sake of producing outstanding health care outcomes is developed in later chapters pertaining to the tools of foresight within strategy formulation and decision making.

Now before us lay the matter of what can be done to remedy the present problems that are very real while also keeping an aim toward the future, so that we and our followers are properly equipped—not simply for a past age but for the one coming down the pike. First, we might consider what tools and ideas are already present among us, specifically when it comes to leadership and organizational interactions. The notion of control is bound up in the discussion of what leadership is, regardless of whether modern-day leadership experts want to say it or not. It is unpopular and politically incorrect to even promote the semblance of dominance or hierarchy in many contexts; but the fact of the matter is when leaders make decisions and delegate work, there is not always a right to disagree without organizational consequences. The military is certainly a proving ground for this reality. Of course, nothing in this book asserts that control is ever to be used for what has been termed "toxic leadership" purposes. Leaders have the right and freedom to use authority for good, never for evil and self-serving purposes. Few would disagree, since leaders generally want those above and beyond them to be equally mindful of their own good.

So how might control be exercised? Three means of control have been considered sufficient in organizational leadership. These are control through information, special influence, and resources. The first relates to the perceptions of high-value, scarce expertise, and insight. Individuals who know something that needs to be known, especially if the information is dynamic and cannot simply be told but must regularly reemerge from internalized understandings, tend to acquire influence. The second pertains to what might be termed charisma, the special, personal magnetism individuals assert through their personality quirks, physical appearance and actions, voice, and interpersonal skillfulness. The third relies upon external resource capabilities, that is, different forms of wealth. Of course, wealth can entail money, relationship networks, reputation, lineage, and more. Ultimately, this third means of control highlights an interesting aspect about leadership longevity. Wealth, in some ways, is a promise of security, of the potential for endurance. Just as fat on the body is a store of energy for the future, so fat in the company accounts is a store of provisions for future needs. However, the kind of leadership that uses wealth uses it functionally in the same way that others use information or charisma.

These three are means of leadership control through scarcity. The glaring oversight is that such models' effectiveness disintegrates when scarcity transforms into abundance, when specialized knowledge is pervasive, when people-decision networks are easily discernable, and when platforms for analysis are accessible and more powerful than previously imaginable. Are we open to such a possibility? Regarding the power of thinking, algorithms exist and are now being created to help replicate the work of the information control perspective. When formerly constrained information becomes abundantly available, expertise becomes further specialized, as renowned economist Adam Smith noted a few hundred years ago. Researchers and practitioners, given such circumstances, become more adept in specific applications of their fields. Thus, specialists abound, but they retain control only within their shrinking domain. The power of general knowledge dissolves into the abundant pool of shared information. Being an expert/specialist loses its broad appeal, since many are experts to some degree.

Regarding resources and wealth, many industries have established the fixed costs and are facing what is considered a cooperative economy and compete against digital, zero-marginal cost competitors. Such competitors experience no variable costs for additional uses of previously limited and controlled information or power. Consider how difficult it was in previous generations to ensure a large population knew a particular information. Consider the wealth, and therefore benefactors, needed to ensure the message went out and was effectively communicated. Consider now the available, relatively free access technologies that help propagate such work with little to no cost to the user. In the modern economy, information is potential wealth, potential power. Bartering personal information (in order to access these tools, websites, etc.) is now costless in the sense that it does not require the removal of capital from one's self to trade that capital. You retain your information as much as the recipients gain that information. As for charisma, with the advent of information inundation through Wikipedia, Google, and YouTube, and all kinds of market-leveling technologies, the power of the individual to persuade has been limited. One's influence is constantly compared against the perspectives and opinions of others, which are easily accessible and searchable online. Thus, as soon as an opinion is voiced, its strengths and weaknesses can no longer be hidden from the audience. In that respect, charisma and emotion and previous authority structures are losing their preanalysis credibility; and, the institutions upon which they are established are similar experiencing crisis.

As this pertains to health care, it should be obvious that patients have far more power and authority to search the Internet and voice concerns and questions across social media today, in formerly unavailable ways, that help or hurt them. The situation where a doctor's diagnosis is all there is to go on is no longer the reality clinicians face. Given that Google Voice or Apple's Siri can try and answer a medical question with the whole Internet (and we have not even mentioned IBM's supercomputer Watson), clinicians are experiencing incredible pressures to their long-established institutional authority that cannot be lightly dismissed.

A Future Among Many

Scarcity paradigms may no longer be tenable, at least not in the way formerly utilized. Essentially we face a dilemma: The conclusions previous paradigms offered are no longer given. Our structure for certainty has been shaken. The paradigms we need, then, must be able to help with our inherent reliability question—a question of how reliable is your perspective compared to mine in this matter, X or Y. In some respects, this is the prevalence of postmodern thinking patterns replacing modern thinking patterns. In the modern era, much like clinical examination structures, a clear delineation for diagnosis and execution of remedies exists. A key tenet is the notion that all issues can be diagnosed through this system with acute expectations. In postmodern thinking, multiple pathways might exist, but there is certainly a larger system of issues that may not be illumined by the normal diagnosis and application of remedy cycle.

Just like truth is a whole, so we are now rediscovering that health is too. What this means for organizational leadership contexts is far-reaching.

It means that the expectations of clients may be shifting from pragmatic understandings that, health care intends to solve my momentary problem of pressure/pain and then step out of my life to the more holistic understanding that, health care intends to help direct my life toward better health. But, old paradigms do not aid in perceiving this kind of change within the industry and without. For that kind of insight, thinking more about the larger, cultural future is central—rather than thinking simply about one organization's future in its target market according to temporarily stable assumptions. As Eric Dent wrote regarding the worldview shift that complexity science wrought upon the world, "if an organization experiences changes more rapidly than it can comprehend and control them, then it is not possible to keep the system stable."[3] This perspective leads us to think of the challenges we face as issues to manage rather than problems to which we can find solutions.

Would you not agree that the future—yours, mine, and our industry's—seems to be up for debate more than in previous eras? This follows the modern-to-post-modern jump, from assumed clarity to assumed ambiguity. The jump itself, as discussed, is not so much an indictment that we have forgotten things we once knew as a society (though there may be truth in such a charge); instead, the jump is related to the overwhelming awareness that our understanding is now recognized to circumscribe only a small ring of knowledge within an inexhaustible body of information, pulsing throughout the cosmos. And here you and I are simply dealing with health care—how quaint.

One issue we face is that of information management.

- What matters and what does not?
- How will we know the difference?
- How will we process the difference once we figure it out?
- How much will it cost to gain that capability?
- What is the likelihood that our new paradigm will falsely count insignificant something the old paradigm would have picked up?

---

[3] Dent, E.B. 1999. "Complexity Science: A Worldview Shift." *Emergence* 1, no. 4, 5. Business Source Complete, EBSCOhost (accessed on March 3, 2019). 10

One obvious question about the future, in our approach to strategic planning, is: how great are our expectations of certainty versus certitude? The former pertains to plain prediction and the latter deals with our confidence levels about explicit or implicit predictions. The new paradigm of pervasive uncertainty argues that the latter is more important, because the former is impossible. The old paradigm, however, was unwilling to toss out the possibility of complete accuracy in prediction. Predictive modeling today continues this trend under an assumption that simply by having larger data sets we can approximate reality better. There is some truth to the notion that the closer you get to reality (with more real data points), you approximate reality; but, it is obvious that until you have the complete set—described above as inexhaustible—you will not accurately capture the necessary information for a full predictive capability. We must consider the value of a model we know will never do what we would like for it to do.

Why is this discussion important? The answer is that we need strategies for our health care systems that take the very real complexity of reality into account. The changing nature of our markets demands strategies and organizations flexible enough to shift in more than just matters of resources. The old strategies that relied upon leadership of information expertise, charismatic presence, and resource wealth cannot be expected to have the same impact. Yet such strategies should not be discarded. The present-future is far more complex and nuanced than to suggest wholesale expulsion. We need to consider present evaluation of those old paradigms and consider their merger with what we find emerging.

In consideration of emerging concerns about Social Security, Medicare, consumerism, obesity, aging populations, immigration, digital information repositories, cybercrime and identity theft, and environmental issues, the idea and practice of innovation needs discussion. This is part of the powerful replacement strategy to fill in the gaps created by emerging changes that have already stretched old paradigms to their limits. In a sense, we need new wineskins for the new wine. No matter your industry, no matter your position, and no matter where you have gone in the past decade, you have been persuaded that innovation is good. Innovation, in that regard, is a key component in competing for the future, where organizations are more like ecosystems with interstate connectors between stakeholders than isolated ships at sea.

Introducing the Model

Rare is the individual who is blind to how greatly innovation has helped improve life with access and speed. Given a generation that needs both improvement and the integration of new and old, innovation acts like an instruction manual for positive change. In many ways, they are functionally synonymous in our vernacular. Thus, innovative leadership models—which are what this book is all about—illustrate the art of crafting positive change in the ambiguous and dynamically changing environment. To give you a glimpse into the latter portion of the book, it involves anticipation and foresight processes and practices that posture leaders differently in how they need to consider "time" and its affect upon their work of leadership—especially regarding envisioning the future and "preparing" for would-be surprises. Later discussion will couch these concepts within the field of strategy, as foresight and anticipation are constructs operating upon and within the strategic capacity (though many of us have them set to "silent," running in the background, but never checking their updates).

In the chapters ahead, understanding where change in health care is headed, how innovation is mixed into the concoction, why the essence of strategy and its substrate foresight are significant to the leadership portfolio, and the manner of fitting it all together will be made plain. Chiefly, the argument herein is for a threefold application of leadership practices, each circumscribed by a particular kind of leadership paradigm.

1. The first is built on the anticipation and foresight concepts. This kind of leadership helps identify the reasoning for innovation and offers some signals as to what direction an organization can take given how the macro environment affects the meso (industry-level) environment. For us, this primarily pertains to the U.S. health care system, but the concepts can certainly be applied for other industries. In fact, keeping a broader perspective is *more* likely to

provide a better ranged view of the future for the sake of more robust innovativeness.

2. The second application of leadership practices deals with strategic choices once the anticipation and foresight practices have been applied. Such leadership is less long-range compared to the former, but it is more specifically oriented to decisions an organization must make with the next few years in view. The market will change quite a bit, to be sure, but the odds are in its favor that it will not wholly cease to exist, that is, there is far more structural integrity to the paradigm used for strategic leadership than for anticipatory leadership.

3. The third set, considered herein as administrative leadership, is near-term leadership of the practice management sort. Ideally, this kind of leadership helps create organizational space for future innovation by identifying and leveraging efficiencies. When the organization can use fewer resources to compete at the same level or higher, there is a possibility of reallocating the saved resources for new purposes.

Summary

A leadership portfolio as argued for above engages a whole innovation cycle from conception through production and into renewal. *This is integrated delivery of leadership: the execution of a cohesive portfolio of leadership practices that promote outstanding health care outcomes.* As a portfolio, leadership is no longer locked into one diagnostic for organizational health and remedy; rather, leaders have at least three *concurrently* operating diagnostics in the form of the leadership practices and the assumptions undergirding the long term, the medium term, and the present. Furthermore, leaders should find they have more flexibility with this approach to leadership because of how it properly balances the competing needs of present efficiencies, medium-term choices, and long-term contingencies.

For health care leaders, the winds of change are familiar and often noxious. I hope this model becomes your breath of fresh air, releasing you from simplistic management efforts or flash visions and providing you with avenues to establish powerful organizational practices for ongoing, long-term, sustainable, breakthrough, and disruptive innovations—the kind that generate real value and help you keep loving what you always imagined health care could be—what we know it should be.

Leadership "Intel" Snapshot

To say that the 1960s were a decade of change would be an understatement. Near the end of the decade, engineering marvels Robert Noyce and Gordon Moore, having already left a company they cofounded years before, decided to double-down and set out on a journey to found another startup. Their story undergirds Silicon Valley's emergence, of Palo Alto, California's significance to the digital revolution, and the reason TED talks are interesting and books on innovation are worth reading. Those were the days of the first rocket ships, guided missiles, handheld calculators, and microchips. With them came the renowned "Moore's Law," and other predictions, scientific discoveries, and technological breakthroughs.[4] Noyce and Moore caused industry shifts that opened doors for wealth creation. However, as happened at Fairchild Semiconductor (their former venture), investors exercised the right to buy the company— meaning control was now in the hands of a boardroom separated from the minds in the laboratories. With the boardroom not willing to incentivize promising engineers with equity opportunities, the organization's momentum slowed, and Noyce and Moore—among others—decided to get off the train.

The two went back to the same financier who had put the Fairchild deal together, and with only three pages describing the men and a few sentences overviewing what their company would focus on—the money rushed in. Why? It was no secret that Noyce and Moore were the Valley's Midas's. This new company, Integrated Electronics Corporation—better recognized today as Intel—would establish that reality more clearly than any other. But, for our purposes, these brokers of the digital revolution did something even more enlightening: They successfully evolved a contextually appropriate organizational culture. To head off any momentary confusion: No, this book is not singularly about corporate culture or

---

[4] These stories are best told by Walter Isaacson in chapters 4 and 5 of his book *The Innovator's*. The history shared here draws much on Isaacson's retelling.

cultural change management, though there are some aspects to innovating leadership that will touch on those subjects. More directly, the leadership elements that arose at Intel from among its various chief leaders, which allowed as well as propelled its success, are necessary elements for all innovation development processes.

History paints the picture best. Essentially, there were three chief leaders at Intel from the beginning: Robert Noyce, Gordon Moore, and their third person, Andy Grove (acting as the director of engineering). In Isaacson's words,

> Moore was ... unpretentious, nonauthoritarian, averse to confrontation, and uninterested in the trappings of power ... Noyce ... could dazzle a client with the halo effect that had followed him since childhood. Moore, always temperate and thoughtful, liked being in the lab, and he knew how to lead engineers with subtle questions or (the sharpest arrow in his quiver) a studied silence. Noyce was great at strategic vision ... seeing the big picture; Moore understood the details, particularly of technology and engineering. [T]hey were perfect partners, except ... with their shared aversion to hierarchy and unwillingness to be bossy, neither was a decisive manager.[5]

In contrast with the other two, Grove was both technically competent as well as an in-your-face manager, a point at which he thought the other two were either incompetent or unwilling to address matters of decision appropriately—with intensity. Grove would later understand the value of their different leadership practices and how they strengthened rather than weakened the company. Isaacson, agreeing with the argument of management guru Peter Drucker that the best leaders were thinking beyond and about the organization while also acting, mentions Grove's insight that the three embodied the whole executive function. In fact, the mastermind financier, Arthur Rock, in an interview with Isaacson, mentioned how significant it was that the three would become CEOs of Intel in the order of Drucker's argument:

---

[5] Isaacson, W. 2014. *The Innovators: How a Group of Hackers, Geniuses, and Geeks Created the Digital Revolution*, 192. New York, NY: Simon & Schuster.

Noyce he described as "a visionary who knew how to inspire people and sell the company to others when it was getting off the ground." Once that was done, Intel needed to be led by someone who could make it a pioneer in each new wave of technology, "and Gordon was such a brilliant scientist he knew how to drive the technology." Then, when there were dozens of other companies competing, "we needed a hard-charging, no-nonsense manager who could focus on driving us as a business." That was Grove.[6]

Interestingly, many of the digital revolution's founders had Judeo-Christian upbringings. For instance, Noyce was raised in a Congregationalist home among a small community, and Intel's beginning highlighted his penchant for nonhierarchical organizational structures. Later, Intel would later assimilate the authoritarian leadership practices of Grove, who was undoubtedly influenced by his Jewish upbringing in Hungary as the Nazis rose to power and transformed the company for magnificent productivity. From the beginning with Noyce, Intel took shape like a collaborative meritocracy. As an example, Noyce used a beat-up aluminum desk in a visible cubicle while new hires were given mahogany, a practice Grove later adopted. Thus, if not Noyce, then no one else was entitled to much at Intel, and so the culture started to take the shape of a meritocracy. Additionally, Noyce prized open communications, readily accessible information without bureaucracy, and personal accountability. These were entirely compatible with the visionary needs and expectations of the organization.

Of course, many others besides new organizations can glean from the Intel experiment's harvest. Moore's approach to deep technological advancement and Grove's passion for execution and top tier market competitiveness are masterclasses of their own. Most importantly, though, is that those three leaders' inclinations toward particular leadership practices propelled Intel to new heights at different points in its organizational maturity. Moreover, some developments renewed the organization's youth. At first, Noyce's visionary leadership kept the organization loose enough to lead the industry's shift and define its

---

[6] Isaacson, W. 2014. *The Innovators: How a Group of Hackers, Geniuses, and Geeks Created the Digital Revolution*. New York: Simon & Schuster, 2014. 192.

long-term path. Theirs was the company setting the industry's agenda, drawing the map.

In charting a course, they needed enough of a view to the environment to determine which technological horse to hitch their engineers to. By the time Moore took the reins, the hitch was set, but what they needed was horsepower. Moore was an exemplary engineer and prodigiously intelligent. His challenge was not so much determining which industry to compete in as much as how to ensure Intel was driving the intellectual gains within it.

Finally, Grove was the leader ensuring Intel maintained focus. Much like a gatekeeper, Grove worked to accelerate the organization as well as put a stop to new efforts that he saw were taking the organization out of its wheelhouse without good reason. For instance, despite their fragile position early on, where their difficulty was in keeping up with business rather than not having enough, Grove recognized the importance to develop the microprocessor (a project that arose in order to help develop special microchips for a Japanese calculator manufacturer), and did not object to the overwhelmingly intensive project. That awareness was key to Intel's future—and the future of the digital age.

CHAPTER 1

The Changing Healthcare Landscape

What's Behind the Door?

The changing healthcare landscape is our first point of contact with the conception of an integrated delivery of innovative leadership processes for the sake of outstanding healthcare outcomes. When we talk about healthcare today, even though we want to be optimistic, we are talking about a system on fire, under fire, and underwater. It is changing, being criticized and condemned, and sinking the nation financially. But, it is also necessary for the public good, incredibly complex in makeup and integration, and one of the best available in the world. Moreover, I think most readers practicing or leading in the United States are proud of what we have built and that other nations prove their systems against ours and train their people in ours, and that we have a unique opportunity to shape the sector's next lap. In that respect, it is better to nourish rather than berate and bury the opportunity. Yet, on the whole, our healthcare system has problems. Those within and without the sector see and bemoan the failures, whether it may be the inability displayed in identifying patients correctly, quickly, consistently, and "fairly;" promoting or obstructing transparency in quality, outcomes, costs, rates, and competitive advantages; or providing quality consistency for service at all capacity levels, to both patients, staff, and additional stakeholders.

As healthcare grows, expectations grow with it. That is the nature of authority's expansion alongside reliance and dependency. The notion that you cannot meet an expectation is often considered for the first time when it happens. The double-edged sword is that we want our stakeholders to believe we are reliable and can meet those unvoiced expectations. Such confidence keeps both parties loyal. Like with romance, there is a level of comfort and there is a level of mystery. Comfort makes us feel welcome, and mystery makes us feel special. But, is it not a bit presumptuous to think we can fool our stakeholders into thinking we are invincible–unless, of course, we have a plan and the resources to execute upon it, proving we at least supersede what they could otherwise expect from the industry? We may not be impenetrable, but we want to give them confidence that we are their best bet, and that is only one of the peaks of success. The chief end is to climb higher than realistic expectations and provide better services across the board for the long run.

Our industry also struggles with matters of fiscal responsibility, expansion, and governmental involvement. Questions constantly surround the institutions of Medicare and Medicaid and the enigma that is the Affordable Care Act. What do these three and their offspring mean for the future of payments, the nature of the insurance industry, how fees will be structured, and whether corporate healthcare will become something other. Of course, as the government becomes more involved, the problem area of public health becomes more prominent. Something that has dominated the European system while the American system has focused on private care becomes far more significant when payments are increasingly subsidized by the taxpaying constituency. Such issues will not be addressed for solutions in this book, as I do not want us to focus on policy as much as on practice. But, it is important for the sake of later considerations of anticipatory leadership: that we lead with our eyes and hearts open to the sounds of cultural angst and policy revolutions in order to rightly navigate our ships in the churning seas of change. Remember, there are only a few productive ways to interact with change: start it, amplify it, manipulate it (redirection) and oppose it. Of course, you can be carried along by it, but you likely do not see that as a leader's best approach.

Pertaining to fiscal responsibility, we are already aware of management practices from big business applied to healthcare operations, which grate against the "do whatever it takes" mentality many have in regard to the healing profession. What we are facing is a radical notion that fiscal concern may have a legitimate place in the waiting room and operating room. For some, this is audacious: that lacking resources could be a legitimate reason for not providing care which is scarce but "available." Certainly, proponents might argue that care is available *on loan*, meaning the organization is indebted for the access until someone comes along who is both in need and can pay (whether on their own or through a policy under which they are enrolled with an insurance provider). In that sense, the case made by proponents is that expensive care resources (the ones which are exhaustible and not just those with high fixed costs and near-zero variable costs which might be depreciated overlong lifespans) are at hand for access but not use—just like banks are nearby and accessible for loans, but only for eligible members. Still, when it comes to life, this seems brutish until you introduce a two-victim, one cure dilemma. Even then, when the life of an organization is considered, and that payments lead to organizational sustenance that supports the care of far more individuals, the reality of having to choose remains a highly volatile, unethical, and predatory paradigm. One thing is sure, we need to affirm that ethics matter, and so in our decision-making and leadership paradigms, we do not want to fall into the false notion that logical, value-creating decision making is ever better by not considering ethics and morals. Ethics, rightly understood, ensure our decisions protect what is truly valuable rather than discard it for things less worthy. Never forget this. It will keep you like a crown on your head.

You Know, It Wasn't Always Like This

Surely you are familiar with the concept of not being able to know where you are going until you first know where you have been, the idea being that self-awareness and destiny are encrypted, and only reflection can help decipher and provide a right orientation for the fulfillment of your potential. Whether you believe that or not, it is helpful to understand the process by which the present state of healthcare emerged. It has taken hundreds of years to progress and entrench itself in the American way of life according to its current structure and systems. In this regard, we would be do best to receive instruction from Paul Starr (1984), author of the Pulitzer winning history, *The Social Transformation of American Medicine: The Rise of a Sovereign Profession and the Making of a Vast Industry*. Starr provides the key components and framework for understanding healthcare's evolution in the States. After he introduces readers to the origins of the concept of professional sovereignty and how authority is structured, he expounds upon how the historical beginnings of medicine in the colonies and frontiers, like in other cultures, was a mixture of religion and womanly wisdom. Bluntly, the work of medicine and well-being was considered a lesser-than role, and it was "relegated" to the work of the still considered lesser gender of women. In some respects, it might have been that men were uninterested on the whole in promoting the field for financial gain, because there was no systematization by which one could assure results of the medical practice. Without that key ingredient—the semblance of authority and expectation—there was little opportunity. In societies where men necessarily would be bread-winners, medicine was not a hot prospect for middle and lower classes, at least not for a little while longer. Until then, the only medical practice with any honor was among the elite nobles for whom the study of medicine was more related to scientific inquiry for the sake of knowledge than the bloody and dirty involvement in the affairs of "common people."

In fact, the American system's change away from that perspective over time due to no small swath of social, environmental, economic, and political changes, helps explain some of the main differences between the American system and the European systems that exist to this very day. Starr (1984) writes,

In early American society, medicine was relatively insignificant as an economic institution. Insofar as care of the sick remained within the family and communal circle, it was not a commodity: It had no price in money and was not "produced" for exchange, as were the trained skills and services of doctors.[1]

He adds, in relation to the nineteenth century's dramatic changes in the field of medicine across America,

The advocates of economic liberalism believed that in the care of the sick...private choice should prevail—hence their support for the abolition of all medical licensing...On the opposing side of the issue, seeking protection from an unconstrained market, medical societies tried to limit entry into practice and commercial

[1] Leavitt, J.W. 1984. "Paul, Starr." *The Social Transformation of American Medicine*, 59. New York: Basic Books.

behavior, like price cutting and advertising…medical aid to the indigent and, after the turn of the century, government and professional regulation of the drug industry. In different ways, professionalism, charity, and government intervention were efforts to modify the action of the market, without abolishing it entirely.[2]

Additionally, the market expansion that occurred included the transportation and communication revolutions, increasing the area of accessibility for medical care. First, this decreased the time spent to make a visit or call, so that doctors could visit and advise more patients per day. Second, this decreased the expense to families who paid the physician fees, which dropped as a result of the first's effect on price competition. Later on, the same forces would have the effect of decreasing costs for patients visiting doctors instead of the reverse. Another expansion factor was that prior to the Civil War, the number of physicians rose faster than the population rate. A driving force of demand was the increasing urbanization that took place alongside the change from agrarian to industrial culture. One result was the distancing of work from the home, which had an additional effect of making it more difficult to attend to the sick within the family. Hospitals emerged in greater numbers in such a climate, for the sake of medical education's growth, the general welfare of the communities and the replacement of formerly low-to-no care locations housing the sick poor, and to meet the demand for new spheres of medical influence among different practitioners who could not find opportunities to reach their medical aspirations among existing hospitals.

Starr makes the case that from after the Civil War until around 1930, the American medical sector underwent a massive shift toward professional consolidation. During this time, he argues that medicine as a profession, distinct in making rules and standards for itself, began a significant fusion process. It took decades and was at times rancorous in nature, as power structures were affirmed or denied. Intense jockeying occurred to determine who would be at the forefront and "on top" after the dust of the field's restructuring settled. To make that work, consensus had to be established, and this struck at the heart of the social class hierarchy which was

---

[2] Ibid., 59–60.

itself present among the ranks of physicians. To that end, the unification most positively impacted middle-class physicians who operated outside of the noble favor of well-to-do institutions that favored particular physicians' heritages. The lower-class physicians, the ones more aligned with pseudo-science—especially as modernism and the emergence of faith in scientific empiricism took hold in the late nineteenth and early twentieth century—began to find themselves further exiled from the community. The middle fought for their place at the table and the upper realized their own impotence to keep professional medicine from collapsing without the middle's support and the lower's removal.

In too simple of terms, the lower-class physicians brought reproach on the field and did not support the emerging authority—displayed in their adherence to unapproved, unlicensed practices. This kept the upper-class physicians' respectability from rising, for their field was one in the same. As it is said, a teaspoon of tar can pollute a barrel of honey. From a field with relatively low incomes to one where incomes progressively beat the average and would later far outstrip the rest of society, status became a major factor in the field's rising importance to American life and how fees and incomes shifted. Starr notes, the shift of great consequence was the one in which the field slowly ceased to be competitive and became more corporate. Citing James Burrows 1963 organizational history of the American Medical Association (*AMA: Voice of American Medicine*), Starr (1984) points to evidence that the number of physicians who had joined the AMA had reached 60 percent of all physicians in the country by 1920, dating that period forward as "organized medicine."[3]

The establishment of medical societies and the large memberships they gathered helped the medical field establish self-regulation and assert itself against remaining competition, specifically the authority of the pharmaceutical makers. Physicians gaining credibility through respectable education apparatus gave way to the doctor as gatekeeper and trusted advisor of health. This increased dependency on doctors resulted in what Starr (1984) called a retreat of private judgment.[4] With the transfer of care,

---

[3] Leavitt, J.W. 1984. "Paul, Starr." *The Social Transformation of American Medicine*, 109. New York: Basic Books.

[4] Leavitt, J.W. 1984. "Paul, Starr." *The Social Transformation of American Medicine*, 126. New York: Basic Books.

best judgment, and authority from the home to the hospital, medicine was primed for a new status at the heart of American society. Scientific developments at the biological, chemical, and technical-tool level forced a wave of advancement upon the profession. And, "by providing more accurate diagnosis, identifying the sources of infection and their modes of transmission, and diffusing knowledge of personal hygiene, medicine powered the improved effectiveness of public health.[5]" Furthermore, the nature of hospitals themselves changed, shifting from communities to approximate more formal business organizations. Starr points out,

> Early hospitals had a fundamentally paternalistic social structure; their patients entered at the sufferance of their benefactors and had the moral status of children. The staff, who often resided as well as worked within the hospital, were subject to rules and discipline that extended into their personal lives. A steward and matron, who might be husband and wife, presided over the hospital family. As the hospital has evolved from household to bureaucracy, it has ceased to be a home to its staff, who have come to regard themselves as no different from workers in other institutions.[6]

Perhaps the most significant change that occurred was that which dealt with the philosophy of diagnosis in general. Prior to the shift in technology and instrumentation, Starr (1984) points out, "physicians depended in diagnosis primarily on their patients' account of symptoms and their own superficial observation; manual examination was relatively unimportant."[7] Thus, over time, the medical profession took on a status of being mindful of and privy to a special class of understanding, which tethered vital information to the complicated operation of particular tools and machines and the difficult and deft interpretation of the tools' results. From the patients' perspective, the separation of diagnosis from either their own (patient's) explanation or the doctor's capability to

---

[5] Ibid, 138.

[6] Ibid, 149.

[7] Leavitt, J. W. 1984. "Paul, Starr." *The Social Transformation of American Medicine*, 136. New York, NY: Basic Books.

observe without aid, promoted a sense that medicine was unquestionably accurate. We can probably see here that such logic is powerful, for you cannot argue with machines that simply perform their task without prejudice. What we did not account for, however, was that such machines only produce results in keeping with our paradigm and only operate according to assumptions upon which they were built. Still, they have had great effectiveness and advanced the field significantly, supporting the healing, saving, and protecting of countless lives in the process.

Hopefully, this brief synopsis of some of the radical shifts that helped construct the medical complex of the twentieth century proves an important lesson as how various forces *will* result in significant industry changes—many of which may be unpredictable. However, unpredictability does not mean devastating or need to be fear-inducing. It does mean we need to have a better eye on what shifts are taking place in society that may or may not have any semblance of direct relationships with healthcare. Just as the telephone and automobile changed the locus of medical authority and venue of medical service from home health to private practice and eventually the rising hospital system superstructures, so too can mobile phones, medical information databases, virtual reality, 3D printers, and other technologies (not to mention social issues!) press forth their own agendas. That kind of awareness is anticipatory, and it should be a crucial component to our leadership docket. Moreover, it needs to be conducted in the right way. Many can say they keep abreast of issues and monitor changes in their sectors and some beyond them, but that is not foresight in the sense needed. That is more helpful than not doing anything, but it is insufficient to be considered a profitable leadership practice. We will discuss that more in chapters 4 and 5. First, we will first look at where leading experts believe the industry is headed. From their launching pad we can make headway toward a responsive strategy.

The Map Says We Are Here, but Where Is *Here?*

I present the following findings from credible analyses of the shape of American medicine in 2015 and what that might mean for how much was changing and has changed since. To start, we will consider Bain and Company's *Front Line of Healthcare Report 2015*, which pointed out from its survey of 632 physicians across specialties and 100 hospital procurement administrators in the United States, that:

- There has been a noticeable shift toward management-led organizations by physicians who have changed employment,
- Emergency medical record (EMR) use had dramatically increased, along with treatment protocol use,
- Some areas within the country are susceptible to a faster pace of change than others (citing Massachusetts compared to Mississippi and Alabama respectively),
- Physician satisfaction is significantly higher toward physician-led organizations compared to management-led organizations,
- Physicians believe their organizations' procurement officers are more influential in deciding which devices are used and drugs are prescribed, to the effect that physicians feel constrained,
- Where pharma sales reps were formerly critically important sources of information a few years ago, it would seem they are only important for medical divisions with increasing complexity and innovation; however, in markets where the pace of change lags behind, they remain generally vital,
- And finally, physicians believed the unmet needs of the future would be best supported by medtech and pharma companies already having the strongest category leadership (meaning the company's market and the physician's specialty align).[8]

The survey-centric findings encouraged Bain to make arguments for several generalizations about trends in the healthcare arena. One, that, "the financing and delivery of healthcare is becoming more systemized," likely turned heads (2015, 1). The onset of and ongoing longevity confusion regarding the Affordable Care Act, the notion of accountability and consolidation through cost-controls, specifically in the form of

---

[8] Bain & Company, Inc. 2015. "Front Line of Healthcare Report 2015: The Shifting US Healthcare Landscape by the Numbers." http://bain.com/Images/BAIN_REPORT_Front_line_of_healthcare_2015.pdf. ii–4

centralized and aggregating structures and processes, has forcefully taken ahold of what used to be permitted autonomy. In some respects, this seems to amplify the evolution that congealed the field of medicine since the mid-1800s. *The shift in leadership from trustees to physicians to administrated systems is something old, not new.* But, the force of the change, supported by technology and shifting social conscience, which can make it even more acceptable, is.

Our second bellwether is the Health Research Institute of PricewaterhouseCoopers. They offer industry leaders, "new intelligence, perspectives, and analysis on trends affecting all health related industries."[9] In their December 2014 report, *Top health industry issues of 2015: Outlines of a market emerge,* which was based on a commissioned survey of 1000 U.S. adults about consumers' viewpoint of the healthcare sector along with their healthcare usage preferences, they shared Bain's perspective about technology's force in changing the quality, speed, and cost of healthcare. They showed how Millennials, in particular, are forcing changes with their preference to have healthcare coupled with their technological comfort. Along with this is the reality that consumers demand more control over-healthcare offerings: They are shouldering more cost-responsibility, both directly through personal expense and indirectly through the tax-based subsidization of welfare recipients. Such personalization, the Health Research Institute report argues, is leading healthcare to become both more mobile, so that patients have anytime access to individualized information and consultation with medical staff when either is away from the office, and also more commoditized, since transparent pricing is what consumers expect when they have to put more of their own money on the table.

Continuing with the theme that healthcare market is being driven by regulation, cost control, and technology expectations, Vaughn Kauffman and Trine Tsouderos of the Institute, in their February 2015 article for *strategy +business,* "The Future of Health is More, Better, Cheaper," noted how streams of consumer convenience culture along with cost

---

[9] PwC Health Research Institute. 2014. "Top Health Industry Issues of 2015: Outlines of a Market Emerge." 12. http://pwc.com/us/en/health-industries/top-health-industry-issues/assets/pwc-hri-top-healthcare-issues-2015.pdf.

consciousness are merging into the healthcare industry. One can easily look at the newest mobile operating systems and their partner devices to understand how integrated healthcare and technology have become. In one sense, consumer devices have become an extension of preventative medicine through the lens of personal awareness. Consumers of this kind of technology are now aware of their own personalized medical information in highly intelligent ways at fractions of the cost of visiting a practitioner's office (at least monetarily and temporally). Moreover, always-on, always-connected devices put even highly specialized medical information at consumers' fingertips. This is the overlay of a pull-market on top of a traditionally push-market. Physicians used to push far more information and care to patients. In turn, patients pull care from physicians and healthcare organizations because they are now customers. Formerly, one might have called the physician-patient relationship something like a patron-client relationship, where the patron supports the well-being of the client and the client respects and adheres to the guidance and commands of the patron. They were not equals. Hierarchy was obvious, with authority and responsibility vested in the patron. The current change has left the patient both with more authority and more responsibility. Simultaneously, the physician's role in both of these categories has diminished, causing tremors in the younger generation's aspirations toward and perceptions of the field. We know that perceptions guide decisions, and most of us have known both the benefits and consequences of good and bad perceptions. Consider how an organizational attribute like being known to have an excellent care-driven culture can affect the future, to the point that employment applications increases (more job-seekers aim to capture the value of being within the organization), turnover of valuable employees decreases (seeking to retain and increase their value-capture), and more top-tier physicians desire to work there and are recruited because the environment begets appreciation. Value stands out, demanding to be captured, but more on that will be discussed below.

The Relationship Question

These kinds of preferences (mobility/control) on the consumers' end are influencing payers to demand more cost-savings from providers, since the fee-for-service model encouraged providers to offer patients the care desired—at a certain price to payers. This is leading payers to demand better proof of outcomes from providers' services. Essentially, there is more demand for more, and for some, more means more, and for others, more means less, that is, this is a triple-constrained system in its current form. Consider these contributory relationships:

1. Patients' freedom to participate [or not] in the healthcare market-place is decreasing, increasing their personal costs, and so patients are demanding more control in return.
2. Providers' freedom of operation is decreasing proportionally with increased regulation, increasing their personal costs, and so they are also demanding "more," sometimes in the form of less responsibility for patient relationship-development.
3. Payers are facing greater competition with patients' choices and competitive offerings increasing, decreasing their margins and increasing required oversight on providers.

This is a cycle of constraints, where the patients are putting pressure on payers who are putting pressure on providers, where providers' pressure is venting into the application of care itself. Furthermore, one could argue lobbies for providers and payers and patients are all pressuring governmental agency for their cause, further muddying the waters. Since the waters are yet to settle, and the promises from the 2016 and 2020 US presidential elections and their powder kegs of political fallout have even still yet to fully accrue, one cannot say how much more pressure the system will support before an imminent change: collapse, incremental adjustment, or transformation.

What can be known is that mobile-connectedness is creating access—to consumers and competitors. Consumers may be local, regional, or beyond, and competitors likewise. Thus, markets are both growing and shrinking, product categories the same. This is the little-big world we are a part of and in which we have to strive for excellence and success. Electronic medical records (EMRs) are one of the game-changers that seek to deliver value on the mobility and access promises. But, with innovation integrating into established markets comes transformational pain, the discomfort stemming from changes that occur in order to manage present difficulties. Like merging onto a highway, with one party speeding up and another momentarily slowing down for safety's sake, the old and the new must play nicely for a short time before a new normal presides in the environment. With the access and mobility EMRs have unlocked for patients, EMRs have also caused numerous difficulties for information securitization. Increasing record accessibility means just that: it is far easier to now access patients' records—even inappropriately. In one respect, the savings from this transaction cost (transferring records) that EMRs have unlocked has shifted to the market of cybersecurity. Thus, information technology is becoming exponentially more important in competitive healthcare organizations, as much for administration as for clinical staff.

Another major driver of change in the healthcare sector is population change. Healthcare is an imminently people-oriented sector. In the April 2014 report "The Next America," PewResearchCenter author Paul Taylor illustrates the monumental social shifts that have occurred during the past half century among the U.S. population. From perspectives on marriage and racial equality to confidence in government and optimism about the future fiscal health of the nation, the research illustrates the irrepressible force of social change at work. Yet, the fact that the Baby Boomer generation (listed by Taylor as those U.S. Americans born between 1946 and 1964) is larger than previous or succeeding generations has meant that its paradigms and perspectives have had a powerful impact on the current shape of the country—and that future social change will have to aggregate multiple generations to oppose Boomer paradigms. In fact, this is what happened in the 2012 U.S. Presidential election, where younger cohorts were much more disproportionate in their young/old partisan voting gap.[10] Tying in the younger generation's familiarity with technology, the report shows how those under the age of 50 were far more comfortable with (or had a desire to engage in) Internet social networking than their elders. In one sense, this was an indication of technological comfort, but in another sense it also begged the question of how social interaction was changing, along with transparency of information and

[10] Paul. T. 2014. "The Next America." *PewResearchCenter*. http://pewresearch. org/next-america/#Two-Dramas-in-Slow-Motion.

social familiarity. For healthcare leaders, social change can mean regulatory change, which is occurring in the United States. More specifically, this is also having profound effects on payer mix. As governmental statutes affect patient coverage, providers are being tasked with burdens both in terms of who they must provide care for as well as [by payers] what that care needs to look like. Thus, some are wondering if the days of the independent clinician are over, to the effect that some organizations are attempting to gobble up whomever they can (independents and groups), increase the authority of administration within their models of organizational leadership, and leverage economies of scale in negotiations with payers.

How to Count Wins

This brings us back to the dilemma of cost-effectiveness and transformation for the sake of greater fiscal restraint within the sector. It would seem—momentarily—that gains are reduced through the new burdens. That, however, would only tell a bit of the story in the aggregate. Perhaps the question needs to be better parsed as to who benefits most from these changes, as that will also highlight who seems to be doing most of the guiding of healthcare's future. If we consider the system noted earlier about patients, providers, and payers, then we would see that payers seem most powerful. Truly, we may view this kind of system as bolstering the notion that he who has the gold makes the rules, yet that would be too simplistic. Why? Because, patients are consumers who are also holding purse strings; and, providers have been cooperatively savvy since the early twentieth century to offset payers' power—as much through professional as well as through nonprofit lobbies. Without being too mercenary in our perspective, we see how operative the fiscal concern is to every player. This constraint is pressuring each player to find new ways to create slack for themselves, whether through decreasing costs or increasing benefits. Ultimately, these are exchanges of value, and so winning entails value creation. Since the fiscal unit is simply a store of value, strategic efforts often seek to increase margins in this category, but one could just as easily count wins as improving speed of delivery, which creates the opportunity to capture more value in the same amount of time. Another restructuring of "winning" might be delivering equal care with fewer operating assets in play (think mobile technology or nonphysicians providing care traditionally restricted to physicians). Still one more would be the establishment of strategic partnerships and alliances that can bring value in the form of greater access to necessary technical assets, extend market reach, and efficient system integration (among other advantages).

Summary

Since no one knows the future, the interaction of these forces remains uncertain to a high degree. Each participant's choices will corporately shape how the future of healthcare in the United States looks, and since most players are advantage-seekers, few will dedicate themselves to strategies that are inflexible—and even more may take up a wait-and-see posture, expecting others to test market hypotheses for them. But, the clarion call for innovation is unavoidably powerful, especially amidst uncertainty. Those who can successfully innovate within an upended market have a great chance to capture value that is no longer loyal to a particular capital flow, the reason being everyone is on the lookout for more value. And, more choices are resulting in players having a great opportunity to reevaluate their value-capture process. Thus, once one player shifts, at that moment his signature to the rest of the market changes, and like a domino effect, the whole market may shift in turn to reposition their own offerings. Healthcare leaders need to observe this semblance of control over market shifts that innovation seems to offer. Clearly, control is advantageous. But, even more than observe, as healthcare leaders, the best choice would be to identify a means of practicing this method of market self-determination through the implementation of innovative processes. To do that, however, one first needs to understand innovation itself, the subject of the next chapter.

CHAPTER 2

Innovation as a Cure-All

Have you ever wondered about how comfortable modern automobile drivers have it? These days you can push a button and your vehicle can maintain constant speed, adjusting acceleration for the terrain. It may not be the safest button, but it sure is helpful for long drives on relatively uncongested highways. Several years ago, the gentleman who holds the patent (Daniel Wisner) was awarded at an alumni banquet at my alma mater. He has some other great patents too, one having to do with the electronics undergirding antilock brakes. Daniel and other men and women like him seem to have a special manual, the "bring it to life" manual. You see, these innovators understand that solutions need more than ideas. They need more than inventions. They need innovations. According to the Product Development and Management Association (PDMA) glossary, innovation is, "a new idea, method, or device. The act of creating a new product or process. The act includes invention as well as the work required to bring an idea or concept into final form."[1] Similarly, innovation scholars and expert practitioners highlight the effects of innovation's ability to, "create new value at the intersection of business and technology."[2] Truthfully, despite what one may have heard, innovation is neither exclusive to high-tech gadgetry nor a mystical output of enigmatic "creatives." Moreover, while it acts as a boon to organizations, it is not a resource that must be acquired in abundance at all costs—despite what

---

[1] PDMA. 2007. "The PDMA Glossary for New Product Development." *Product Development and Management Association,* Available from http://onlinelibrary. wiley.com/doi/10.1002/9780470172483.gloss/pdf, 591 (accessed on April 3, 2015)

[2] Davila, T.M.J. Epstein, and R.D. Shelton. 2013. *Making Innovation Work: How to Manage It, Measure It, and Profit From It, 29.* Upper Saddle River, NJ: FT Press.

the hype artist on the magazine cover shouts. We have all read articles threatening doom and gloom unless we take drastic measures to avert calamity. Most of us are not in that position, though it may not take long to fall into the hole if we neglect the options innovation-making presents to us.

Innovation is best understood in clearer relief, measured with regular business management tools and otherwise mundane functioning. Certainly, innovation would not be the subject at hand if it failed to be a chief lever in sustainable competitive advantage (a topic addressed in the chapters 3 and 6). Even progressive improvements that cause no seeming commotion today could be considered as tomorrow's catalytic innovations, redefining industries and shaping the business models of our future. Again, the point is to capture value. Additionally, there are numerous ways to classify and categorize innovation. To start us off, we need to further stratify the concept of innovation, looking first at sustaining and disruptive innovation and then at incremental, semiradical, and radical innovation. In expanding our conceptual vocabulary, we make it easier for ourselves to plan, lead, and evaluate our innovation work appropriately. The health care space is massive, spanning so many people, products, and processes, that it would be easy to confuse innovation as a certain kind of thing that is only done in one small quadrant. If we think of innovation as highly technical, then we might assume it cannot apply to a seemingly nontechnical practice. Again, from a bird's-eye view, innovation is about bringing an idea, method, or device to life. Basically, a more effective means of checking the pulse or method for physicians to wash their hands can be considered innovative, though it may be of a different kind of innovation when compared with social networking or online education.

Please Be More Specific

First, there is the notion of sustaining and disruptive innovation, developed by Clayton Christensen of the Harvard Business School. Sustaining innovations refer to the outputs of organizations that build upon what already exists. They are not separating from nor at odds with the preceding generation of products, ideas, or services. They advance it in a logical way, whether in minor *or* major fashion. For instance, "some are simple, incremental, year-to-year improvements; others are dramatic, break-through technologies, such as the transition from analog to digital and from digital to optical."[3] This is incredibly instructive. For health care, just think of imaging machinery. Even when we shift from one kind of imaging to a more powerful kind, we are still operating in a competition where more powerful equipment requires greater resource investment (either in the system or in the operator), and our goal is simply to image a target quickly, cost-effectively, and with greater clarity.

In contrast, *disruptive innovation relates not to the gravity of a breakthrough; instead, it pertains to the innovation's impact upon how competition was determined prior to and after the innovation's emergence.* In an interview with Mark Smith, Christensen provides the following definition:

> A disruptive innovation is a technology that brings a much more affordable product or service that is much simpler to use into a market. And so it allows a whole new population of consumers to afford to own and have the skill to use a product or service, whereas historically, the ability to access was limited to people who have a lot of money or a lot of skill.[4]

Essentially, disruptive innovations change the rules of the game by which the industry plays. For that reason, newer firms have greater flexibility to leverage this kind of innovation, while the reverse is true for incumbent organizations. The idea here is that larger organizations already leverage assets cost-effectively and use existing processes and strategies for sustaining innovation, whereas newer, smaller, organizations will not have the same kind of access to capital. Since those newer and smaller firms do not have such footing in their industries' current competitive environments, they have greater flexibility to attempt to usurp their markets by changing those rules. If successful, when new firms get a footing with traditional market customers, they can eventually creep into

[3] De Kluyver, C.A., and J.A. Pearce II. 2012. *Strategy: A View From The Top.* 4th ed, 128. Upper Saddle River, NJ: Prentice Hall.
[4] Smith, M.D. May 2007. "Disruptive Innovation: Can Health Care Learn From Other Industries? A conversation with Clayton M. Christensen." *Health Affairs* 26, no. 3, 288–295. http://content.healthaffairs.org/content/26/3/w288.full

the incumbents' marketspaces with their innovations. At that point, the market is disrupted because the innovator entered with a new way to win the space that is presumably better in matters of cost efficiency or nonprice value. Were that not the case, the upstart would have simply adopted the original manner of competing and sought to squeeze out additional efficiencies or win in some other sustaining innovation manner. To continue with our illustration about imaging equipment, a disruptive innovation would not look like the sale of more powerful machines, but it could pertain to a new model of device usage, which focuses on breaking the boundary of constraints that keep the industry focused on more powerful device creation. For instance, an innovator might make an argument for some new technology that identifies the same information (or more robust information) differently, arguing their method is better (cheaper, safer, easier to employ, less technical, etc.). Perhaps this new technology does not follow the notion that images and sight are as accurate as some other indicator that this new machine can display. An existing health care example that Christensen discussed in the interview was LASIK surgery. His argument was that as the competency to perform the procedure became embedded in the machine rather than the operator, the field of "vision improvement procedures" was disrupted.[5] For clarity's sake (no pun intended), it is possible for new entrants to become sustaining innovation winners, but it is just that such an opportunity favors incumbents who know the rules and how to navigate them better. In one sense, the multifaceted innovation process is like a reinforcing loop, as the innovation process begets innovation attempts from incumbents and additional entrants alike (but not equally), like a game of leapfrog. In another sense, it is like a balance-seeking loop, where sustaining innovations become cost-prohibitive for new entrants or even for the market itself, encouraging disruptive innovations to make an appearance, shaking up the innovation cycle as the old paradigms lose value and the new paradigms capture and create it.

[5] Smith, M.D. May 2007. "Disruptive Innovation: Can Health Care Learn From Other Industries? A Conversation with Clayton M. Christensen." *Health Affairs* 26, no. 3, 288–295. http://content.healthaffairs.org/content/26/3/w288.full

Second, Davila, Epstein, and Shelton offer three additional classifi-
cations for innovation—incremental, semiradical, and radical—to help
us grasp the work of innovation.[6] Unlike Christensen's descriptions
of sustaining and disruptive innovation, which illustrate the effects of
innovations after the fact, these categorizations teach how to construct
an innovation. To start with, these categories relate to how the innovation itself is a mixture of technological and business model change. For
example, incremental innovation pertains to what you might consider
the general improvement and development approach, which the three
authors cast in the mold of typical problem solving efforts (We need more
X—where an increase in X is the traditional industry solution), and so
only minor change needs to occur in either the area of technological or
business model innovation. This kind of innovation work typically results
in a sustaining innovation. Again, the difference between the two is that
incremental innovation relates to the construction of the innovation
itself, whereas sustaining innovation relates to the results of an innovation
on its competitive marketspace. To that end, incremental innovation is
a vital tool of incumbent organizations seeking to leverage their long-
term investments in particular proprietary technologies, long-standing
partnerships, knowledge capital of employees, legal and regulatory allowances, And, within the field of innovation itself, its importance should
not be downplayed. We might consider it to be the bread and butter
approach to innovation, often absorbing, "more than 80 percent of the
company's total innovation investment."[7]

Furthermore, we need to be careful about assuming the direction of
innovation, as one could incrementally innovate through a reduction
in quality as a means to decrease the cost of a product or service. This
is called bargain innovation, and Nelson, Cohen, Greenberg, and Kent
explain how, beyond health care, this has been a successful strategy among
customers—even when it has put their lives in jeopardy—explaining,

---

[6] Davila, T.M.J. Epstein, and R.D. Shelton. 2013. *Making Innovation Work: How
to Manage It, Measure It, and Profit From It.* Upper Saddle River, NJ: FT Press.
[7] Davila, T.M.J. Epstein, and R.D. Shelton. 2013. *Making Innovation Work:
How to Manage It, Measure It, and Profit From It,* 42. Upper Saddle River, NJ:
FT Press.

Consumers have been comfortable with many decrementally cost-effective options outside of health care that pose morbidity or mortality risks. For example, automobile manufacturers produce many vehicles that lack certain safety features (for example, side curtain airbags), because some consumers are willing to forgo those options to reduce the purchase price.[8]

As health care leaders, we need to keep a very close eye on such practices, because even if that kind of strategy could help garner additional revenues from some particular target market, it would also undoubtedly disrupt confidence levels among current consumers of our health care services. Such a dilemma is where strategic perspective comes into view. Using the example of the automobile and safety features, consumers may be willing to give up value stemming from the safety component additions and accept a more uncertain transport, since consumers and even marketers tout safety as a luxury attribute, an option. In health care, however, the quality of care provided is an expected, core attribute, just like the capacity for forward motion in a vehicle. Even if one organization promises a higher level of care, the notion that care will be intentionally lowered is a foreign concept to many consumers of health services and to clinicians as well for that matter. It is something of an undocumented assumption that less qualified clinicians are not working in the highest quality organizations. That is to say, we do not tend to believe practitioners would limit their abilities; instead, we only believe they reach their potential. To some extent, this is how we accept less costly, seemingly less than excellent care. Still, this ties into the earlier discussion about cost reduction in health care. Such innovations highlight the value of cost reduction to almost every sector, as there will generally be a larger market comprised of those who cannot afford them or find the financial burden a primary decision criterion than there will be those who can afford them or pay little attention to the cost of quality at its highest "bleeding edge" prices.

---

[8] Nelson, A.L., J.T. Cohen, D. Greenberg, and D.M. Kent. 2009. Much Cheaper, Almost as Good: Decrementally Cost-Effective Medical Innovation. *Annals of Internal Medicine* 151, no. 9, p. 665.

In contrast to incremental innovation, semiradical innovation calls for a more substantial adjustment to one of the categories (technology or business model) with little adjustment to the other. In regard to what pressure points we can touch to innovate, we find three for each. For technological innovation, we can change the product or service directly, the process by which we manufacture the product or service, or the support structure undergirding the previous two. For business model change, we can shift the value proposition of a product or service, the method by which the product or service is created and delivered, or the intended consumer. Thus, a semiradical health care innovation would take into account a significant change to one of either category—such as a change to the delivery mechanism of a specific medical device along with a minor adjustment to the device's value proposition. However, while semiradical innovation can shape the competitive landscape in ways incremental innovation cannot (like customized care options being offered within a traditional health care organization), radical innovation reframes the product or service entirely, like an à la carte, online-only organization. Notice that such an idea may not seem like it could capture a large market and become overtly competitive. It would still be a radical innovation, however, since the term relates to the changes in technology and business model rather than market changes. Both are technologically dependent types of change (each requires some change to both categories), where semiradical *may* be heavily technologically supported and radical change *must* be.

On that subject of technological change, innovation becomes a bit more nuanced, specifically with reference to disruptive technologies. Davila, Epstein, and Shelton note, "Disruptive technologies are a type of semiradical technology innovation, brought about by changing the technology basis, but not the business model."[9] Thus, a significant shift in one of the three technological pressure points listed above can help in the creation of a disruptive technology (like major changes to a medicine's formula or delivery mechanism, the machines and process by which it is

---

[9] Davila, T.M.J. Epstein, and R.D. Shelton. 2013. *Making Innovation Work: How to Manage It, Measure It, and Profit From It.* Upper Saddle River, NJ: FT Press.

manufactured, and/or the supporting workforce and know-how by which the manufacturing is accomplished).

To be clear, then, disruptive innovation is a matter of how the competitive landscape changes due to innovation taking place—it answers the question of what wreckage an innovation leaves behind. Either it sustains the marketspace, or it disrupts it. Either competition maintains the status quo or calls for a revolution among consumers in deciding among options. In contrast, the terms incremental, semiradical, and radical, in relation to innovation, are descriptive terms for the innovation method and type, the mix of business model and technology changes from which the innovation is birthed.

Knowing the Process and the Rules

Other ideas and categorizations of innovation exist, but we do not need to explore that territory at the moment. Once your organization has decided to pursue an innovation strategy, then you can and should investigate the available pathways more rigorously. But, even then, knowing *what* innovation is remains different from understanding how to achieve or create it. When it comes to recognizably innovative ideas, products, and services, there are many historical champions to think of, whether it be Apple, Google, Tesla, GE, Ford, Amazon, eBay, ExxonMobil, McDonald's, The Cleveland Clinic, Johnson & Johnson, Wal-Mart, or others. To join such ranks, organizations need innovation to work for them precisely because these winners are too large and agile as incumbents to compete head-to-head with them. For that reason, organizations seeking to innovate need to understand innovation as a strategy. As mentioned previously, incumbents hold greater market leverage. Those which seem to have regular success with new products and services may simply have a better *innovation process*, and when it comes to innovation strategy, that is a primary goal. Before we get to goals, however, let us consider starting points, and the starting point for grasping innovation strategy is understanding how organizations compete.

Michael Porter and his work on *Competitive Strategy* is a staple for grasping the give and take of market decision making. In relation to Porter's analysis of the typical trade-offs of core competitive strategies (i.e., positioning for top value, lowest cost, or a best-value proposition), Deloitte director Michael Raynor, in his book *The Innovator's Manifesto: Deliberate Disruption For Transformational Growth,* explains the competitive space with the productivity frontier, an economics concept that relates cost position against nonprice value for boundary determinants. Essentially, for a company to increase the nonprice value of their goods or services, they have to be willing to accept higher cost structures and vice versa. This is a trade-off experience that ensures organizations remain distinct from one another, since in order to imitate an organization's full strategy, another organization would have to imitate the former's complete set of cost structural trade-offs, which is most often more expensive (in financial and nonfinancial costs to the company). Among the trade-off options, however, organizations have a significant amount of freedom to improve effectiveness (they can teeter-totter along the trade-off spectrum). And, only those sets of trade-offs that exist along the curve itself (and not underneath it) represent true peak efficiency. Moving onto the current curve or along the curve is simply a matter of increasing efficiency to reduce costs without reducing value or of increasing value without increasing costs. Innovations of all types—even incremental—shift the entire curve outward according to the innovating organization's business model. That's transformative innovation. Then, when competitors adjust their technology and/or models to catch up, they establish the other points along the new frontier curve.

An innovation strategy, therefore, is about breaking through the current productivity frontier. Here is how to use the terms for mapping our market. Nonprice value refers to the key measurement of value for a firm, industry, or market. It might equate to portability, potency, durability, capacity, rarity, or relate to something like outcomes of operations and recovery time, etc. As mentioned, firms can increase nonprice value with efficiency efforts, but once they reach the limit of such efforts, then they face the barrier where costs are necessarily at the lowest possible level, and the only manner of increasing the relative low-cost position is to reduce the nonprice value. This is not the same as bargain innovation, which would change the competitive offering and fill out the frontier curve. Thus, innovation occurs to break the trade-off experienced (either cost or value given up to gain the other) and create a new frontier curve where a product or service's nonprice value can continue to increase without the former constraint of relative cost position (i.e., move further right on the graph without the technological constraints of the marketplace forcing it to move up and left) or do the same for reducing relative cost. While a curve entails innumerably diverse positions for trade-offs, in reality, there are not innumerable competitors. Moreover, innovations—incremental through radical—are regular occurrences, with technological developments occurring asymmetrically across industries.

Regarding strategic opportunities, think of strategic as related to sustained focus on the different competitive options available—through finance, capabilities, and people—in comparison to other firms for the sake of capturing value. We would be remiss to think that we can go about innovation without strategic intent and succeed as often as we need in such a rapidly changing environment—particularly during the present health care reformation. On the bright side, there is great reason to believe that innovativeness is a competency that enables an organization to continually exert breakthrough force on their industry's productivity frontier, maintaining an edge against competitors. To relate this matter to our categories of sustaining and disruptive innovation, we would have to assert that the above is simply sustaining innovation at work, since the notion of competitors along the same frontier having the capability to catch up to the new frontier is an assumption of their own incremental innovation adoption. Thus, when a disruptor emerges and breaks the technology–business model mix, automatically breaking the cost-value mix for the competitive landscape, the only means for incumbents to survive is to compete along the new paradigm, and since that paradigm was not their creation, their adoption only functions as a competitive maneuver but not as a disruptive innovation itself.

General Guidelines for Implementation

The innovation literature has much to say about how to make the innovation strategy work. Generally, the key areas of emphasis are strategic models of approach, management systems for implementation, and culture development. Harkening back to the earlier discussion on innovation mixing business model and technological change, remember that

Davila, Epstein, and Shelton said innovation in either is dependent on three levers, which are the determinants of change for that aspect of innovation. For business model innovation, these were the value proposition, the supply chain, and the target customer. For technology innovation, these were products and services, process technologies, and enabling technologies. The former set looks at how innovation would affect *what* is sold and delivered to market (value), how it is made and moved to the right place (cost), or who ends up with it (value). The identifiers of value and cost illustrate what pulling those levers does for the organization's competitive position in the marketspace. The first pressure point changes the item in terms of the nonprice value axis, since it shifts the proposition by which the product or service is marketed, expecting the new proposition will increase the consumer population's demand and subjective valuation. The second pressure point changes the relative cost of the product or service through advances in logistics strategy. The third relates to the market mix and who is or is not being targeted as a consumer. The latter set of pressure points look at whether the technology change relates to the product or service itself (generally value), the process of the product's creation or delivery (cost), or the decision-making tools affecting all of the above. The first deals with shifts along the nonprice value axis, since it generally assumes advancing the technology of the product or service, increasing its market value. The second relates to relative cost position as it assumes advances from product order capacity and speed of processing (which can move beyond arithmetic efficiency advancement) to those in resource attainment, allocation, production, and/or delivery among others. The final pressure point relates to the system of decision-making tools by which leaders are doing their work, and so it can affect either axis, resulting in faster and better organizational decisions. Faster decisions can mean cost reductions and better decisions can mean value improvement, and both are desirable.

Before explaining further, I offer some innovative technologies that are shaping up on the frontier of the field. Leaders should be capable of recognizing these kinds of innovation and mapping them relative to one's own industry position. To start with, remember that discussion of LASIK surgery as an innovation that, through cost reduction over the past several years with the aid of better equipment that relies less heavily on the expertise and experience of machine operators, has disrupted the arena of corrective lenses. Well, there may be a new disruptor to the field by the name of the Ocumetrics Bionic Lens.[10] Dr. Garth Webb is the founder and CEO of the technology company that has developed a bionic lens to replace your biological lens during an outpatient procedure that claims to correct vision to a multiple of three times better than perfect vision (20/20) after an eight-minute surgery. These lenses never decay, so cataracts are a bygone issue. Furthermore, there is no burning of corneal tissue with lasers. Though there are more clinical trials in order, one can easily understand why eyesight—something we all prize dearly—is routinely experiencing technological innovation. We want to see clearly for our entire lives—at all distances—and we will reward those who succeed in breakthrough developments.

Next, let us consider a development from the field of pharmaceuticals, where an engineering group focused on antifraud technology, has developed a barcode that can be built into a pill's physical structure—too small for physical identification, but visible to laser scanning.[11] The demand for such an innovation comes from the World Health Organization's concern overmounting seizures of fake products, even estimating that more than half of the tested batches of medications purchased online from illegal sites (where many consumers attempt to find cheaper alternatives to domestic pharmacies) were counterfeit.[12] These are not only dangerous to the consumers, but they damage the trusted infrastructure of medication procurement itself. Of course, there are already some existing technologies to check medication legitimacy, but this new technology from Sofmat Ltd. is supposedly the first to affect the physical product. Its success in other materials like plastics proves its concept and value. If found easy to apply

---

[10] Bains, C. 2015. "Ocumetics Bionic Lens Could Give You Vision 3x Better Than 20/20." *CBCNews,* http://cbc.ca/news/technology/ocumetics-bionic-lens-could-give-you-vision-3x-better-than-20-20-1.3078257
[11] University of Bradford. 2015. "Fighting Fakes With the First Integral 3D Barcode." http://bradford.ac.uk/mediacentre/news-releases/three-d-barcode.php
[12] World Health Organization. 2012. "Medicines: spurious/Falsely-Labelled/Falsified/Counterfeit (SFFC) Medicines." http://who.int/mediacentre/factsheets/fs275/en/

and utilize, cheaper than alternatives at scale, and effective at combating counterfeiting, then this could very well shift the entire medication market and decrease overall costs of competition among pharmaceutical producers and distributors.

Another example involves protecting human memories from Alzheimer's and combat damage with the support of government funding through DARPA (the U.S. Defense Advanced Research Projects Agency).[13] The technology is a brain implant that has special software mapping the brain's connections. When memory loss occurs from concussion, injury, or special deterioration, the misfiring that results in failed memory retrieval can be bypassed according to prior mapping. Essentially, the translation that normally carries the memory from storage to access could be skipped by the implant's support. Currently, the technology allows researchers to read the initial signals and output signals (like if/then statements). Then, with the algorithm based on that data compiled, researchers have predicted with 90 percent accuracy how new signals would be translated. If they are capable of predicting perfect translations, then implants could do the work of long-term memory storage for us in the future, limiting the debilitation of disease and injury. Notice how innovation is also introduced by players beyond the industry.

Finally, we will look at an innovation in transaction cost reduction. Researchers from Johns Hopkins performed tests with a hobby-sized drone carrying blood samples for test flights of various times less than 40 minutes in duration to see whether the samples and test results would be affected.[14] Their preliminary findings showed that samples and tests were not affected, meaning the speed and cost of transporting samples for testing (not to mention sanitation!) from hard to reach or quarantined areas could be dramatically improved. Thus, their innovation involves the utilization of an existing technology to address an adjacent field's need

---

[13] Cookson, C. 2015. "Computer Algorithm Created To Encode Human Memories." *Financial Times*, http://ft.com/cms/s/0/466bf22e-66a8-11e5-97d0-1456a776a4f5.html

[14] EurekAlert! AAAS. 2015. "Proof-Of-Concept Study Shows Successful Transport of Blood Samples with Small Drones." http://eurekalert.org/pub_releases/2015-07/jhm-pss072815.php

for a purpose that ultimately changes the trade-off compromise in place. These technological advancements, of major and minor effect within the vast field of health care, only brush the edge of how much technological innovation is currently being attempted within and from without the sector. What is less certain is whether any of these attempts will make deep inroads to shape the future system. Regardless, those who understand what makes up the current system and how it operates will certainly have an advantage.

To prepare an organization for innovative activity, one might first call for an internal and external organizational audit, similar to a SWOT analysis, which inventories strengths, weaknesses, opportunities, and threats. In such an audit, one might consider the technical, organizational capabilities of the firm, evaluate its current business model success, place a value on its funding access and sources, and the coherence of top management's vision. Additionally, one might look to the firm's external network for its capabilities, reevaluate the industry structure, including a measurement of competitive rivalry, and compute the rate of technological change affecting critical industry resources and applications.[15]

After such an audit, and given the issues that arise on the radar screen of leaders as a result, a decision needs to be made: Will the organization pursue what the authors describe as either a play-to-win (PTW) approach or a play-not-to-lose (PNTL) approach to innovation strategy? These strategies attune well with the potential strategic moves outlined by strategy gurus from McKinsey and Company, describing how a firm might act strategically after determining a posture toward the future of a market or industry.[16] The postures toward the future that they arrived at were: shape the future, adapt to the future, or reserve the right to play. The corresponding strategic moves for the postures were: placing big bets, exercising

---

[15] Davila, T.M.J. Epstein, and R.D. Shelton. 2013. *Making Innovation Work: How to Manage It, Measure It, and Profit From It,* 75. Upper Saddle River, NJ: FT Press.

[16] Courtney, H., J. Kirkland, and P. Viguerie. 1997. "Strategy Under Uncertainty." *Harvard Business Review* 75, no. 6, 67–79. *Business Source Complete,* EBSCO*host* (accessed on June 5, 2015).

options, and no-regrets moves. Essentially, innovation aligns with all three postures, depending on whether the organization is an incumbent or startup, and the actions (moves) themselves are differentiating methods to innovation strategy. For example, big bets are future-shaping moves that aim to disrupt the competitive landscape, whereas options are more akin to incumbent investments for the sake of mitigating future risk against disruption. No-regrets movement, in contrast, sustains the innovation track within a marketspace, meaning it generally has to do with efficiency innovations, pushing an organization incrementally toward points on the market's productivity frontier that competitors have not reached (remember the frontier depicts the furthest out places actual organizations inhabit, the graph is only a representation). This would never be disruptive, however, because these moves do not make a breakthrough in the current market's limits and open up the marketspace to an entirely new possibility curve. Most of the current health care innovation going on seems to be found within the latter two categories. Big bets tend to be made by the government with taxpayer monies. As long as the rules are coming from the Centers for Medicare and Medicaid (CMS), it is difficult for organizational leaders to justify big bet outlays of capital, at least for innovations that would be deemed industry-changing. For the moment, it seems most innovation is organization-shaping, industry-aligning innovation.

Firms need to employ the organizational (internal) and industry (external) audit, quantifying and qualifying their competition as well as their competencies in order to craft the best innovation strategy for themselves. Additionally, business strategy experts De Kluyver and Pearce II suggest that product-market strategy considerations add another layer of complexity to the process, noting that, "low-cost leaders often focused their innovation efforts on new production and delivery processes and procedures, while differentiators primarily work on product innovations."[17] By that, they mean technological process and delivery innovations (both dealing with the technology lever) tend to favor upper left innovation, where relative cost position is impacted most. In turn, the nonprice, value-related movements (to the right) typically resulted

---

[17] De Kluyver, C.A., and J.A. Pearce II. 2012. *Strategy: A View From The Top.* 4th ed, 130. Upper Saddle River, NJ: Prentice Hall.

from product and service differentiation strategies, where technological innovations occurred on the actual products or services.

To provide a template for making such decisions and help organizational leaders embarking on innovation strategies get started, Davila, Epstein, and Shelton offer the following action steps:

- "Define the balance of the innovation portfolio you want to see to support the strategy:
  - Mix of business model and technology change
  - Mix of incremental, semiradical, and radical innovations
- Specify how much innovation you want in support of the business strategy.
- Define priorities and trade-offs for innovation investments.
- Clearly communicate this to management team and innovation leaders.
- Repeat until they get it—it may take several times to sink in.
- Conduct diagnostics to assess how well you are doing.
- Ensure that metrics and rewards are supporting the strategy implementation."[18]

Next in significance for bolstering the innovation process after defining the organization's strategic approach are its implementation systems. Some consider this gap the most devastating obstacle we face, and consultants and professors have spilled much ink arguing about the strategy–execution gap. What makes it more difficult is that some experts have affirmed that strategy and execution are separate practices, while others have asserted their integration. No one, however, debates the co-dependency that exists (for strategy that is not executed fails its purpose and execution that is not strategic is poor stewardship), but it seems fair to assert that strategy is the source from which execution draws its power. Alternatively, execution is the purpose for which the power source exists.

To support strategy execution, health care organizations need management systems as complements to their strategies. For instance, with all

---

[18] Davila, T.M.J. Epstein, and R.D. Shelton. 2013. *Making Innovation Work: How to Manage It, Measure It, and Profit From It*, 84–85. Upper Saddle River, NJ: FT Press.

the investment capital needed for many technology innovations, health care organizations at least need to consider how research and development (R & D) fits into their strategic planning efforts. It would be wise for them to develop a resource allocation portfolio by which they can measure and compare their investment in innovation R & D with expenditures and other uses of capital within the firm. Additionally, this could be compared with other public companies' records to the degree of transparency available. The purpose in doing so would be to help them compare innovativeness through spending. The publicly traded for-profits among us will have an easier time finding one-to-one comparable situations with the transparency afforded by required financial filings, but small for-profits will likely need custom measures with financial analysis techniques to generate comparative data. Of course, the goal in comparison is for general, ballpark estimation of the situation, not last-draw, go/no-go decision-making. The R & D system is a means of encouraging the innovation strategy from the angle of technological leverage. Without an emphasis on R & D and capital investment, organizations cannot compete on the technology component of innovation—they will be fast-followers and adopt others' technological innovations at best. Thus, without technological investment (which is not innovation itself), health care organizations cannot engage in radical or semiradical innovation, as both require, at least, small changes in one of the technological pressure points.

Other systems of importance that health care organizations should consider establishing or refreshing—and which need to be used differently depending where along the incremental-radical innovation spectrum they are innovating—include rewards and recognition, project planning, metrics, internal monitoring, process formalization, market research, strategic boundaries, strategic portfolio planning and management, culture, learning tools, knowledge management, partnerships, and external monitoring. Again, systems help with consistent and reliable management of organizational choice and execution, which, for the innovating firm, usually means the management of technology and business model decisions, the pursuit of creative development while also capturing created value, and strengthening and expanding networks while also establishing and leveraging innovation platforms.

Finally, but no less important, is the critical role that culture development plays in ensuring that any innovation strategy emerges successfully. Because innovation is "a product of anticipating, assessing, and fulfilling potential customer needs in a creative manner," it can be won or lost in the strategic planning efforts depending on the health care organization's level of concern for its customers'/clients'/users' needs and preferences.[19] More will be said throughout the next several chapters as we explore the connectedness of innovation to an organization's strategic capacity to intentionally pursue innovation through practices in anticipatory, strategic, and administrative leadership. And, such is co-reliant upon deliberate culture development activities. As organizational culture's role is in the innovation work, cultures without a means of incorporating market turbulence and future demand into their strategic planning efforts will never be purposefully capable of disruptive innovation, though they might get lucky. Thus, an organization whose people are not meaningfully engaged with and whose goals are not attached to shifts in the larger societal culture will have difficulty understanding and responding appropriately to their markets and the kind of demand affecting competitive offerings. Conversely, organizations with strong market research and customer service competencies will have a potential leg up on competitors, with smooth, direct access channels to customer desires, customized and often unintended applications of products/services, and questions. The point of going to such lengths to align with customers is, as Hamel explains, "In the age of revolution, there is simply no way to stay ahead of the innovation curve unless your customers are your co-developers."[20] For health care organizations, this means more than patient satisfaction matters. It means that patient input matters. Front-end engagement is at least as meaningful as back-end evaluation. Restructuring an organization's priorities and practices to extract that outside creativity is difficult for long-standing institutions and takes humility and time. This becomes a strategic advantage for those who succeed. Moreover, quality innovators are freer than their competitors in thinking about innovation as more than hardware,

[19] De Kluyver, C.A., and J.A. Pearce II. 2012. *Strategy: A View From The Top.* 4th ed, 129. Upper Saddle, River, NJ: Prentice Hall.

[20] Hamel, G. 2002. *Leading the Revolution.* Boston: Harvard Business School Publishing.

which is why business model innovation, specifically in the realm of value propositions can be so formidable. One firm that evidences this particularly well is Minnesota Mining and Manufacturing (3M). In fact, the company has its own "culture of innovation" document touting what has made it successful at innovating for the past hundred years. Health care leaders can learn a lot for our industry by seeing how 3M applies and reaps rewards from letting this document drive their innovation-mentality. These include:

1. "Support innovation from R & D to customer sales and support.
2. Understand the future by trying to anticipate and analyze future trends.
3. Establish stretch goals.
4. Empower employees to meet goals.
5. Support broad networking across the company.
6. Recognize and reward innovative people."[21]

3M's mandates align well with what Davila and Epstein argue are key components to *any* innovation culture. They make the point that strategic discoveries are founded in organizational cultures, where, as innovators are resourced and supported (even if mistakes are made or projects fail), innovation is prized (particularly the breakthrough kind). To reiterate, technology need not be the only innovation type considered, because as the risks and necessary resources for innovation are measured, and communication is open and networks are organized, business model innovation becomes especially rewarding.[22] To that effect, I have argued elsewhere describing how culture, transformational leadership, and organizational design are all high contributing factors to effective innovation.[23]

---

[21] De Kluyver, C.A., and J.A. Pearce II. 2012. *Strategy: A View From The Top*, 4th ed. 129. Upper Saddle River, NJ: Prentice Hall.

[22] Davila, T., and M.J. Epstein. 2014. *The Innovation Paradox: Why Good Businesses Kill Breakthroughs and How They Can Change*, 143. San Francisco: Berrett-Koehler Publishers Inc.

[23] Stehlik, D. 2014. "Ultimately Contingent: Leveraging the Power-Web of Culture, Leadership, and Organization Design for Effective Innovation." *Journal of Strategic Leadership* 5, no. 1, 10–22. http://regent.edu/acad/global/publications/jsl/vol5iss1/stehlik.pdf

Summary

So let us ask, why did it matter to learn about innovation again? First, from the previous chapter we have seen how the health care sector has changed, continues to change, and exists within a larger society of ongoing change. In a sense, there are currents of change flowing in various directions, some stronger than others, and health care leaders must navigate their organizations through these waters. There is no alternative; we can simply oppose the waters out of fear, let the waters carry us to ill or gain, or harness the waters for strength in pursuing a course we care about deeply. To the degree that we are concerned with leading successful, patient-centered, society-building, stakeholder-edifying organizations, the first two options are not available to us. If we want to be our sector's change agents that push the limits of quality to another frontier, that import life-saving technologies (and also time and money-saving), that recharge and reward our top performers and keep them growing, then we must chart the path. No one will do it for us. In that vein of thinking, we need to be concerned about innovation. They are nearly one-in-the-same goals. Whether we accomplish our goals by incrementally pushing the possibility frontier of quality and relative cost incrementally or radically, whether the effect upon the industry sustains the current trajectory of effectiveness or disrupts it for far greater gains at much reduced costs, we still require innovativeness to permeate our approach to health care. That's why this chapter was written—to first acquaint us with the vocabulary of innovation so we think and talk and write about it accurately, to second guide our understanding of how innovation works so that we can imagine its application to our work, and to third prepare our thinking about innovation's relationship to strategy and leadership (the subject matter for the next two chapters) so that we can grasp its larger import to organizational success.

CHAPTER 3

Strategy to Win the Future

Perhaps you were like me growing up, and every once and awhile you played board games with your friends and family (more likely a console or computer games in the last twenty years). It was a fun experience—at least until someone started winning, and then the fun stopped and the mercenary negotiations began. Of course, I am only half-kidding, for everyone has a shrewd friend who simply will not let you gain an advantage by trading his ore for your brick or selling you that last property before you can place houses. Games, given their diversity of goals, provide us with a chance to creatively switch paradigms. In some games, we complete tasks, in others we reach a destination, in still more we outlast opponents. In the same way, our approaches to organizational strategy are constructed paradigmatically. For example, if our dominant metaphor is a traditional multiplayer control and conquer game, then success is established by winning tactical engagements, and winning means beating every other player. If our metaphor is a mountain, then it means climbing to the top; a race, then it means being the fastest to cross the finish line; an apocalypse, then it means survival. As our contexts shape our purposes, our goals will be contextualized and in turn help inform our strategic efforts. Thus, what you understand your purpose to be as a health care organization leader is necessarily affected by how you perceive your role in context. That, in essence, is the root of strategy. For instance, if your role is likened unto an orchestral conductor, then your purpose will be different from and your strategy will look different in comparison to a leader who envisions himself as a sage. The former sees his purpose as bringing beautiful harmony out of diversity whereas the latter sees his purpose as providing opportunities for deep insight. The former may see strategy work as a means of increasing connectedness, bridging gaps, and combining strengths, while the latter sees it as his work of expertise and private mental labor revealed in enigmatic rather than clear direction.

The Strategic Management Trinity

The term "strategy" originates from a Greek word inferring generalship.[1] The Greek philosopher Aristotle spoke of generalship as attaining its purpose in victory.[2] So, from the beginning, the paradigm for understanding strategy is competitive. Additionally, from the military connotations it carries, strategy is also an overseeing and directive work entailing greater perspective and broad, long-term vision. In the professional and academic literature on strategy, you will find the field split between paradigms of prescription and paradigms of description. The former consider strategy as something you create, and others consider it something that is observed and reflected upon. The one is known, divisible, controllable, and acted out, while the other is less tangible and is something sensed and pursued. Experts agree that different contexts call for identification with the various paradigms, and that leadership and organizational learning ultimately reshape strategic activities in real time. Aside from that distinction, however, you will find three identifiable practices contributing to the field of strategy (or strategic management). These are strategic thinking, strategy development, and strategic planning. Depending on who you read and what their goal is, the terms themselves or just their definitions may be different, but they tend to be understood as a framework for strategy's congealing. It happens as broad, well-informed conjectures with sound-reasoning become supported identification of best paths, which are organized into a process for deliberate enactment. So we find strategic management as a progression conveyed by the three, from general to specific, from loose to tight, from start to finish, from uncertain to definite. None of the three is suited for separation from the trinity. They exist as a whole, but they operate in different spheres with different immediate goals. To bring this to bear on our previous discussions about the changing health care landscape and how innovation must

---

[1] French, S. 2009. "Defining 'Strategy:' Creating a Common Language of Business Terminology. Emerald Group Publishing Limited." *Strategic Direction* 25, no. 4, pp. 9–11.

[2] *Nicomachean Ethics*. (350 B.C.). (W.D. Ross, Trans.). Retrieved January 25, 2013, from http://classics.mit.edu/Aristotle/nicomachaen.1.i.html

play a major role in our organizational missions for the sake of present and future stakeholders, we must realize that strategy is a forward-leaning posture. The conjectures originating with strategic thinking consist in the realm of the "not yet." And, if we are honest, that is often the response we would give if asked whether our organizations have reached our desired level of success, quality, and effort: "not yet." For that reason, it is the starting line for strategic management, as it forces us to explain why and probe for reasons.

Strategic Thinking: Interpreting the Present

In order to adequately prepare for the future of health care—that space where innovation's blueprints are discovered—we must engage in the work of strategic thinking. Strategic thinking relates to viewing and analyzing a situation from various perspectives for the purpose of understanding it holistically, being attentive to the changes occurring therein for proper action and reaction. This kind of work, however, demands greater open mindedness and creativity than many of us are prepared to provide, especially those of us with Western backgrounds. For this reason, it is important to make sure we understand the differences between strategic thinking and the latter two activities of strategic management. Far too often, people believe such are all iterations of the same thing or have the same goal. That is false. Strategic thinking broadens, whereas strategy development narrows, and strategic planning establishes. To illustrate how these can be confused, consider these remarks from foresight researcher Paul Raimond. He offers an explanation of how cultures—including your organization's—may limit (or release) the effectiveness of strategic thinking, concluding:

> Studies such as those by Nonaku and Takeuchi suggest that Asian companies make better use of creative imagination strategic thinking. This may be a core competence that gives them a competitive advantage. Western companies...use left brain analytical thinking substantially more than right brain creative imagination in their strategic thinking. The Western manager's toolkit of strategy techniques contains far more analytical left brain tools than

it has techniques for promoting creative strategic imagination. That imbalance may be counterproductive. Strategic management needs to generate energy, commitment, creativity just as much as it needs analysis and quantification.[3]

I share this to remind you that strategic thinking is a creative work, and so if you desire to engage the strategic management process correctly, then you need to give yourself the space to be thoughtful and creative rather than single-minded and critical during this work.

To that effect, it is proper to introduce to you (perhaps for the first time) the work of strategic foresight. As it is a primary component to strategic thinking, understanding it conceptually and technically will help establish a base for thinking purposefully and insightfully. For this, we can do no better than by considering the "generic foresight process framework" synthesized by foresight expert Joseph Voros, whose advancement of the technical practice has been an immense help to me and many others in the fields of strategy and organizational planning.[4] In a pivotal 2003 article in the journal *Foresight*, Voros shows how incomplete foresight leads to incomplete, shallow, and/or narrow strategy development and planning. But, to explain why this tends to happen, he first explains what a robust foresight process framework looks like. Borrowing the insights of other strategy and business experts, he points to the existence of three phases that build out the strategic thinking activity. The first is the acquisition of inputs, the second is the core strategic foresight activity, and the third is the extraction of outputs.

Phase 1: Acquiring Information

The first phase is one of aggregation. Gathering inputs is the work of strategic intelligence, and so in this phase the person or team involved in the strategy work identifies shifts in the macro-environment through direct or indirect observation and research (STEEPLE: Societal, Technological,

---

[3] Raimond, P. 1996. "Two styles of Foresight: Are We Predicting the Future or Inventing It?" *Foresight: Exploring and Creating the Future* 29, no. 2, 213. doi: 10.1016/0024-6301(96)00010-6

[4] Voros, J. 2003. "A Generic Foresight Process Framework." *Foresight* 5, no. 3, pp. 10–21.

Environmental, Economic, Political, Legal, Spiritual, etc.,). The team might also hold roundtable discussions about relevant and timely events and note personal experiences related to the present future. This is a generative activity. It creates and does not diminish, with the aim of supplying the observable information created by the internal and external circumstances. It is an accumulating activity, where quality matters, but quantity is expected to ultimately inform the quality of later phases. Thus, during your input phase, you might identify:

- How many competitors in your health care niche exist in your region?
- How many have an online presence?
- Which demographics among your patients are most/least loyal?
- The timeline of regulatory changes that affect your mission,
- The status of the financial environment,
- Changes in payer mix,
- Relevant mergers and acquisitions, and
- Workforce-related changes internally and at-large, among others.

Among foresight practitioners, this kind of work is often called scanning of one form or another, drawing upon the image of radar used on battleships, which pings when an object moves within its range of capture. In essence, scanning is an activity you and your team of leaders can practice regularly by asking everyone to be mindful of what they are seeing and hearing is going on in the field and especially in their areas of practice. You want to routinely be asking, "What is going on?" and have the built-in organizational response where everyone is expected and prepared to report tangible observations. The next phase of foresight can commence once the work of input acquisition has been accomplished.

Phase 2: Strategic Foresight

Strategic foresight, which is foresight accomplished toward a larger strategy effort, is a process of transforming the inputs from the previous phase into the outputs of the next phase. This is accomplished through a series of steps that Voros titles: *Analysis, Interpretation,* and *Prospection* (14).[5] Each step asks probing questions of the information with the aim to generate understanding about the macro-environment in which your organization exists. Again, this is all related to the information collected through your strategic intelligence and scanning efforts. To the extent, then, that your prior efforts are robust, so too will be your capacity for foresight. The Analysis step is your first attempt to comprehend what meaning the information holds, and so it tends to be full of organizing techniques. The reason for the information requiring organization is that the inputs are simply data points with no connections, and the appropriate analysis techniques for this first step are those which help generate easily identifiable connections and patterns. For example, you conduct trend analysis at this step, as it would help you and/or your team quickly identify any observable patterns from your inputs. For instance, you might recognize increasing, decreasing, cyclical, arithmetic, and geometric changes in quantities that you observed. You might separate documented events into a table where events are ranked according to their impact on your organization, and then look for additional commonalities among those highlighted events. Moreover, you might already have a monitoring system in place by which you are following the progress of important regulatory issues, and in Phase 2 (Analysis), you could take the Phase 1 data and consider whether any of it would present conflicts for or amplify the trajectory of those issues. Where Phase 1 produces raw information, Phase 2 is all about producing understanding. It starts light in the Analysis step, but then it shifts to deeper levels of confidence and critical thinking.

In the Interpretation step of Phase 2, you engage in systems thinking activities, which may mean the development of causal diagrams or driving forces models, for the purpose of getting to the heart of the context, uncovering the reasons for environmental behaviors captured in Phase 1. Though I would assume most you have heard about systems thinking because of your involvement in health care, if you have not, then there is a simple way to explain it and its goal. To begin, consider how the human body has been categorized by systems (endocrine,

---

[5] Voros, J. 2003. "A Generic Foresight Process Framework." *Foresight, 5,* no.3, pp. 10–21, 14.

circulatory, nervous, and so on). These systems contain parts that work together to produce specific results on an ongoing basis (supplying the body with essentials, cleansing the body of toxins, notifying the body of changes, and so on). Each grouping of organs within its system, functioning properly, exhibits the proper system behavior. We know this because the outcome of the proper behavior is health. When health deteriorates, however, we understand that there is an issue in one of the systems because the behavior is wrong. It may be a single organ's weakening that disrupts the entire system's performance, and once we identify that single issue, we have the potential to reclaim the entire system's performance. This is the power of systems thinking: By shifting the behavior of pivotal components, we can ultimately affect the performance of the entire system in which it operates. Thus, the value of this kind of critical thinking is to identify strategic leverage points in the overarching systems that are relevant to our sector.

Like a military aims to capture geopolitical chokepoints in order to control the inflows and outflows of a theater of war, so also being aware of what really makes the environment tick can give you a competitive advantage in the third step of Prospection. This word, of Voros's making, is the work of crafting compelling alternative futures. It is where your team starts to forge arguments about what could happen in the future—based on their findings from the second step, where what makes the environment tick (and therefore what aspects of the present are most pregnant with the future) is revealed. To accomplish this step, the team could develop scenarios, practice visioning, or even employ backcasting techniques. If you are unfamiliar with these foresight practices, they are fairly well documented and systematized in the academic strategic management literature and have modified iterations among the popular press, and so I will not get explain their specifics. However, as long as you are thorough in conducting Phase 1, and the first and second steps of Phase 2 are reasonably attempted, then you should be able to generate plausible arguments that logically connect your research, analysis, and suggested potential futures.

In order to ensure they do not get off-track on this step, it is essential that you remind your team that this is not a prediction session. Predictions are readily dismissed in the conjuring and rarely accurate, making it all too easy for team members to be critical and deny the likelihood of "predictions" based on their experience or preconceived expectations about the future. Prospection, in contrast, is not prediction, it is not some kind of prophesy by which one knows events ahead of time. It is an act of showing potential linkages between the present and what comes next. Explaining it in this way to your team, you can help them see the multipath potential that the present encapsulates, from which many kinds of futures might break forth. One tangible way to build Prospection familiarity is to take the systems maps that might have been constructed in the second step and see which components of the system are most vulnerable to change given your scanning results from Phase 1. Then, with those vulnerabilities identified, team members can consider together how various changes to those leverage points might affect the overall system's behavior. In so doing, they are building the narrative structure of a plausible future. The quality of these alternative futures are as useful as they are logically consistent (not meaning with regard to their predictive accuracy). The key to this logical consistency is the degree to which the image of the future created is both believable and originates from good input data. Thus, it is equally a matter of high-quality storytelling and high-density and high-quality observations.

Let me try and explain the strategic thinking process—up to this point—allegorically. Imagine there is a full barrel of puzzle pieces. You do not know how many pieces are in the barrel or even if all the pieces ultimately fuse to create the same picture when placed together; nonetheless, you are tasked with identifying what is on the face of the pieces to the best of your ability. You are able to take as many pieces as you want, but you have to be able to reach into the barrel and grab them on your own, as there will be no help given. After you have taken the number of pieces you are capable of or comfortable with, you then begin to arrange then as best as you can. You check for similar-sized pieces. You separate them by colors, straight edges, patterns, thickness, type of material construction, and so on, Then, depending on if they are from what seems to be the same or different puzzles and based on whether any can be fit together, you start to list assumptions about why the groupings exist. Perhaps one has large pieces that may be a children's puzzle, and alongside the colors or portions of visible words and characters, you make some reasonable guesses about what the entire image could be. If there are other pieces remaining of a seemingly different set, then you attempt to do the same with the other pieces. You take your guesses and reasons and lay them out as clearly as possible for your audience, perhaps even making multiple separate arguments for the same set of pieces (where the divergence does not originate with the pieces themselves, but with the assumptions about what those pieces depict where it is not abundantly clear).

Phase 3: Output Extraction

Phase 3 of the strategic thinking process relates to taking the work from the previous phases and extracting out the insights you and your team generate. So far, you have manifested a great amount of information, answering questions about what kind of environmental data exists and which of it seems important enough to keep abreast of, how that information can be understood and what it means (that is, what story is the environment really telling), and also about the potential role this information could play in how the future environment turns out. That work done with the inputs, in essence, was strategic foresight. The next task in the strategic thinking process is to take what strategic foresight generated and mine it for relevant insights. These will be of two forms, the first of which is readily understood by most leaders in the form of an actionable list of strategic options. This is generally a list of tenable solutions to address the plausible futures from the foresight work. The problem here, however, is that we were clear from the beginning that such futures are not predictions, and so options to leverage those futures should not be understood as strategic in the actual future. There is no way of knowing. To avoid this error, leaders need to be mindful that the value of strategic foresight in strategic management is to ultimately test the resiliency and flexibility of the strategies you have in place and those you craft against the plausible futures your team can generate. By engaging in this kind of work, you can be more confident in your team's ability to produce strategies that are more adaptive and less brittle when future surprises smash against your expectations, the kind of bombshells our organizations never plan for. To reiterate my point, insights in the form of lists of such options are good—as far as they are used correctly. They have importance less in their surface recommendation and more in their underlying assumption about how we and our organizations needs to adjust for change, and the kinds of actions we could take if desirable and/or necessary.

The second form these insights take is just as true but remains less concrete. These kinds of insights compare to the first as an observation of a whole system compares to identifying the color of a single object within that system. In effect, this form of insight is related to the team's perspectives and paradigms and how those shift over the course of Phases 1 and 2. It would be proper to argue here that strategic thinking practices promote strategic thinking. The immaterial output of the scanning and foresight work is the new paradigm participants gain from the process, the realization of change's tangibility and intangibility, the manner of extrapolation and interpolation by which we can gain both deeper perspective into the present and an expanded and extended view of the future. Voros tells us this kind of output "is undoubtedly the more important form of output because of the way it alters the very mechanism of strategy development itself, namely the perceptions of the mind(s) involved in strategizing.[6] Of course, the first form of output is still of great importance if the kind of foresight work is applicable to the participant's work from the start. The reason I mention this is many foresight exercises engage information outside of the participant's field in order to get them accustomed to the foresight process. With such a different kind of thinking being promoted by a foresight workshop's facilitators, the argument goes, to try and teach you the process using the domain you already have the most firmly fixed and well-reasoned assumptions about would be like fighting an uphill battle. Ultimately, however, it is ideal, and you learn the most from and through foresight by practicing it within your own domain.

Strategy Development: Decisions, Decisions

Clearly, strategic thinking does not *simply* precede strategy development. It does precede the development practice, but it also permeates it and follows it. The phases previously described illustrate how strategic thinking

---

[6] Voros, J. 2003. "A Generic Foresight Process Framework." *Foresight 5*, no. 3, pp. 10–21, 15.

contributes to the strategy development and planning (to follow) practices, but the key insight behind these practices is that after they have been initiated, they should be ongoing. They follow in sequence, but the sequences are adaptive and iterative and cyclical across organizations. When one division or unit in your organization is forming its strategy after completing the development work, another may be gathering new inputs and planning from previous strategic thinking and development work. The process advances with clear order the first time, but afterward, these practices continue—to some degree—asynchronously. Certainly, we have to sync up our strategies and budgets across the organization, but we also need to be attentive to the trade-offs made when we sacrifice the best process on the altar of agreed scheduling. Where there is legal requirement, the choice is made for you, but within the bounds of the law and financial obligations, the better way (method) is the best way.

As to the practice of strategy development, this is the first practice of taking the insights gained through strategic thinking and applying them to your organization's actual strategic issues. For example, suppose you have been crafting and implementing yearly or multiannual strategic plans for a while, and during your output phase of strategic thinking the group identifies some highly probable environmental factors that, if occurring, would seriously disrupt your plans and put the organization under enormous stress. This insight is then brought to the table of the strategy development workers—who are usually a subset of leaders who participate in the strategic thinking work but have more responsibility and accountability for the organization's decision-making success and failure (whereas the strategic thinking team should be highly diversified across as many organizational domains as possible). These leaders would take the existing strategic plan, which identifies the strategic goals of the organization (the output of this development work), to determine whether those goals remain the intent of the organization and should continue to be pursued, and to what degree. The vital importance of having a team continuously engaging the strategic thinking work cannot be overstated because of the separation between the two kinds of teams for strategic thinking and the work of development and planning. As the decision makers separate from the organizational "antennae," the capacity to make decisions attentive to internal and external environmental change diminishes. Keeping this link thriving will ensure the strategic decision-making work of development is well watered with the source of its power, for the kryptonite of strategic decision making is inadequate and/or untimely information.

If we must set a linear path for strategy development, since that is how we tend to think of development, then the initial segment would be establishing the criteria for decision making itself. Decisions, to not be arbitrary, must be rooted in some agreed-upon values by which the leadership team can accept or reject them and also rank them accordingly. In essence, strategy development is about answering the question "How will *we* prepare for the future?" Thus, the input–foresight–output process of strategic thinking organizes the boundaries for making a best approximation of what will matter to our stakeholders then and the transformation that gets us there. The strategic assumptions we hold about our own resources (tangible and intangible), however, grant us added constraints. In health care, we can immediately assert the regulatory and reporting constraints limiting our strategy development. Next, we can also identify ethical and reputation constraints inherent to our industry. We are a do-good industry. There is no getting around it and remaining competitive. Mercenary health care is something of an oxymoron, and we would do best to avoid any identification with it.

Much of the initial process of defining the organization's mission, vision, values, and goals (MVVG) is well-published within business strategy bestsellers. Perhaps that means we do not really understand it as a leadership society—or we think it would be great to spend the necessary time on them but the marketing department or firm we hire will complete the work more expediently. We can always look back to the reference books anyway—as if that would help us. Truly, this kind of MVVG framework strengthens your organization's posture in the way that a skeletal system gives structure to your body. It is far from sufficient for life, but it is necessary and has great purpose for everything involved. In fact, this set of decisions is the first step in creating a strategy portfolio, which might be best seen as a set of concentric circles for which the innermost circle, the core, consists of these chosen directions (who we are, why we exist, what motivates us, and what signifies success, and so on) for your organization.

Ginter, Duncan, and Swayne describe a chain of logical strategic decisions along these lines, beginning with those just described (which they call directional strategies) and continuing with adaptive, market entry, competitive, and implementation strategies.[7] The last of these pertains more to strategic planning, and so I will put off its description for the moment. Basically, the purposes undergirding each strategy exist within the next innermost ring. Thus, the implementation strategies would be a means to accomplish the ends of competitive strategies, which functions as the means to the end of market entry strategies, which functions as a means to the aim of adaptive strategies, which exists as a means to enact the directional strategies.

To explain, consider your organization, and, assuming you already have directional strategies in place, the strategic chain mentioned above would have you first determine whether expanding, reducing, or maintaining the current strategic scope is in order, that is, how broad or narrow the present strategy is. For instance, given what you know and believe about the healthcare environment you compete in, is greater diversification of products or services in order? How about harvesting gains in a particular division before expected stagnation hits and the costs become too great to maintain the division as users shift to other options (especially if disruptive innovation attacks)? Or, is it too risky in your team's opinion to attempt any more adaptation, opting instead to simply enhance the current strategic plan?

After these questions are answered, the next set of questions would pertain to purchasing, cooperation, and market development strategies, with the intent being how to enter into a new market, assuming this aligns with the strategic intent of the previous adaptive strategy (scope). Perhaps your organization needs to join a health care system alliance, raise investment capital for a new venture, acquire some specialty care providers, or license a clinical technology or technique. These are all possible solutions to entering new product, service, and geographic markets. Furthermore, these answers provide the information and purpose behind the strategic posture and market position your organization takes as a competitive strategy. These choices tie in significantly with your organization's level of innovation focus, as strategic postures are predominantly a question

---

[7] Ginter, P.M., W.J. Duncan, and L.E. Swayne. 2013. *Strategic Management of Health Care Organizations,* 7th ed. 210–310. San Francisco: Jossey-Bass.

of balancing stability with opportunity. At one end of the spectrum is the organization posturing to maintain a semblance of continuity and sameness within its market. This is especially true of many incumbent organizations. To hold off would-be competitors, such organizations aim to defend by leveraging efficiency drivers. Within the health care arena, such protectionary measures can be seen in efforts to, "engage in vertical integration to protect their market, control patient flow, and create stability … through penetration strategies and limited product development strategies.[8] On the opposite end of the spectrum is the posture of opportunism. This posture befits organizations that are thoroughly innovative and innovating. Let me immediately be clear: This is a posture, potentially proper at a given state in time to accomplish a specific purpose. Do not think I am advocating something as anti-strategic as a one-size-fits-all strategy, as if that is not an oxymoron. Some characteristics of this posture pertain to the organization's domain. For instance, they fit, "rapidly changing environments or service categories such as health care technology and frequently engage…in diversification and product and market development expansion strategies…[and] divestment and retrenchment strategies."[9]

Between these two ends lay the posture of contextual balance. These organizations mix the perspectives at opportune times, but they do not markedly dominate in either. For example, they might have traits of stability among particular units and opportunity-seeking within others. Because of their inclination to balance, they tend to be fast-followers rather than first-movers, adopting quickly rather than investing heavily in R & D for razor-edge time-to-market margins. They are generally experts in penetration strategies, anchoring their organization's stability in current market strongholds from which they are fiscally sustained, while they establish colonies of opportunity in new markets. Additionally, these postures engage the entire strategy planning process differently (more will be said in the next section), such as the protective posture tending to plan its strategy based on current assumptions, act them out, and then reevaluate

---

[8] Ginter, P.M., W.J. Duncan, and L.E. Swayne. 2013. *Strategic Management of Health Care Organizations,* 7th ed. San Francisco: Jossey-Bass.
[9] Ibid., 240.

the market. The opportunity-seeking posture behaves in reverse, evaluating the market first, then acting on that information, and finally planning based on the initial results.

Finally, after the overarching strategy has been formulated (an integration of the prior four kinds: directional, adaptive, market entry, and competitive) there are decisions to be made for implementation of that strategy itself. While the next section (strategic planning) does share much in common with this section, it could benefit from some advanced discussion here. The work of implementing strategy is the work of adding value to other work, which can be seen in how such strategies either increase value through what takes place alongside service delivery, in what supports the implementation of all the previously spoken of strategies, or in the documentation and association of specific actions with specific responsible parties. The first sort relates to how you add value prior to delivery, at the point of delivery, and after delivery. You might be adding value through your literature that explains your service more thoroughly or in more understandable language to the uninitiated in health care terminology. It may relate to giving patients or other stakeholders a voice through satisfaction marketing or monitoring of operations and efforts to improve quality output. Or, it may be a matter of improved billing methods. These are not comprehensive suggestions, but they do illustrate something that could add value at each phase of service delivery within a health care provider's organization. The second relates to aspects of support functions and organizational culture and structure. Within health care organizations, you can typically expect the roles of finance, human resources, information technology, and administration to be value-adding in the sense of not being related to service itself but supporting transactions. As for culture, like we previously considered regarding paradigms and assumptions, and as will be further discussed in the next chapter, shared assumptions, values, and behavior does much to promote or inhibit change. Thus, those which promote positive change are invaluable. Furthermore, how the organization is structured also plays a major role for every aspect of the organization, one being information sharing effectiveness (a crucial matter when the stakes are high and lives are on the line). The third is about the specific process for executing the comprehensive strategy and establishing unit-level accountability. At this point we turn to the practice of strategic planning, which is responsible for this work of implementation.

Strategic Planning: Step-by-Step Into the Future

Strategic planning is expectation codified. In that respect, it is like an engagement. The end is understood, but not yet achieved, and in the meantime there is a verbal acknowledgment of and commitment to particular behaviors for the sake of safeguarding that commitment and reaching the desired end. At the same time, the outcome of strategic planning (the plans themselves) should not be understood as marriage. The actions guided by strategic planning are the marriage. They are the commitment fulfilled. The plans themselves only codify the intentions and expectations. Because this distinction can be and is often confusing, many leaders disdain strategic planning. They see it as something static and frozen, separated from and occurring outside of real-time events. They see it as irrelevant and arduous. The real world is faster and more complex than complicated plans, and it requires adaptability, which they cannot account for or provide. But, from what we have already discussed, the process described throughout the previous practice of strategic thinking and development is entirely adaptive and attentive to the environment and changing circumstances. In that light, we should be capable of appreciating what strategic planning actually promises. Modern definitions of strategic planning entail defined, formal processes of meetings and discussions that result in determined, "long-range objectives, procedures for generating alternative strategies, and...system[s]," for monitoring the plans when (if) implemented.[10,11] Planning does not entail the production of a cloudy set of highly varied options for further analysis, because

---

[10] Fairholm, M., and M. Card. 2009. "Perspectives of Strategic Thinking: From Controlling Chaos to Embracing It." *Journal of Management and Organization* 15, no. 1. http://people.usd.edu/~fairholm/JMO_15-1_Fairholm.pdf (accessed on March 2009).

[11] Armstrong, J.S. 1982. "The Value of Formal Planning for Strategic Decisions: Review of Empirical Research." *Strategic Management Journal* 3, no. 3, 197–211. ABI/INFORM Complete. Web. January 22, 2013.

that is the work of strategic thinking. It does not cull those options and determine the overarching thrust of the organization, as that is the practice of strategy development. A plan consisting of all considerations for all variables and their risk that could affect it will never exist and it never should be attempted. Plans exist for implementation, for execution. At this point in the strategic management process, the organization needs actions, not options.

Still, you do need to feel comfortable with the level of risk ownership your plan entails. Thus, a crucial feature of strategic management is to ensure you mitigate the risk you can and are flexible enough to adapt to risk-adding circumstances you cannot foresee (or avoid even if you could). It seems to be a misunderstanding of strategic planning, in which it is divorced from the pivotal foresight work of capturing real data and interpreting the past and present context to understand them better and envision futures that might emerge, which has given it a bad rap. We know the future is a moving target, giving off signals for detection, but ever eluding perfect apprehension. But, planning should not be approached as a prediction output. Yes, strategic thinking does take presently available information and portray images of the future, but not as guesswork. As already explained, the work of strategic thinking and strategy development is more about lateral thinking power than prediction accuracy per se. Plans, as they should be, are not brittle paths of linear developments, which, if not followed exactly, will crumble and leave us falling headlong into the void between the present and the future. To that end, consider the following points about crafting high-quality action plans.

The Six Elements of Strategic Planning

Plainly stated, strategic planning is about structuring the initiation and management of the strategy. This occurs by determining and specifying organizational unit objectives, the particular kinds of actions and activities supporting those objectives' achievement, semidetailed sequencing of the activities, explicit acknowledgment of who is responsible for the actions and activities, the expected resource demands of each activity/action, and a signal as to how the plan's progress is measured along the way. These plans need not be and often should not be extrapolated one objective at a time. Instead, it would be wiser to have many units work on their unit-level plans alongside their relevant senior leaders. Then, those leaders should congregate for the full organization's strategic planning work after having first participated in the unit-level planning (cocreating through listening and advising in regard to the overall organizational mission, vision, and constraints, but not dictating or domineering). Again, this is all occurring cyclically, alongside the strategic thinking and foresight work and alongside the codified strategy development.

Purposeful Objectives

As for objectives, they should be clearly related to and reinforce the goals of your organization. If they do not, then they are not strategic and simply use resources ineffectively. Moreover, because the plan has to allow for measurement, the goals themselves need to be particularized into measurable units. If the objective is qualitative, then there still exist means through surveying and interviews to gather qualitative data in a quantifiable way (e.g., so many responses were agree and so many others were neither agree nor disagree). Some kinds of objectives that might be worth considering could pertain to response times, electronic health records and care processes, innovation efforts, and general leadership development. As you consider where your organization needs to be headed, and where it is constrained and forced to head (or avoid), and what kinds of competitive advantages you may have and are seeking to capitalize on, you can more aptly define objectives that can actually improve organizational performance and lead to outstanding healthcare outcomes.

Specified Actions and Activities

Next, you need to identify the actions and activities that should lead to objective accomplishment. For instance, if you have a unit that strategically plans for innovation, and one of their goals is to improve their innovation effectiveness, and one objective for that goal is innovating on an existing procedure, then they might identify actions to engage in such as: research existing uses and variants of that procedure in relevant journals or host a roundtable brainstorming session and discussion to gather additional ideas and document experience with the procedure. You might also look into licensing technologies unrelated to the procedure, which your unit believes could be merged with the existing procedure to generate a faster, cheaper, and higher quality outcome. These kinds of actions illustrate what you will do to achieve the objectives. For clarity, these actions and activities should display logical order, which is why the strategic plan calls for clear sequencing.

Clear Sequencing

Since we expect our planned actions and activities to evidence a logical progression for achieving objective accomplishment, so also should our actions/activities be sequenced according to time. In a moment I will address constraints, but for now remember that *time* is a constraint. Plans that do not recognize the importance and specificity of time are rarely useful. This is another reason strategic planning has received a bad rap. Plans are not timeless. To be timeless, they would have to also be inattentive to the situational context, and that would force them to neglect specificity and the particularity of actions that are useful and advantageous in the present. We want plans that make a difference to our overall outcome superiority. To do that, we have to attach sequences to our actions that are rooted in our present schedules. In our real-time execution, we may fail to meet some of those sequencing expectations, but we should not fail to set them, for that is tantamount to expecting failure.

Without the belief that we can complete most of what we set out to do, strategy itself is a nonstarter. If and since strategy is value-adding only for those who have something to add value to, then strategic planning is only for those organizations and individuals who already produce a good or service of value. You would not be reading this book if that was untrue of you and your organization. I also believe you can establish plans that are realistic and stretch your current performance. Moreover, as you engage this process, your team should become more aware of your organization's capacity to manage time. You will find out over the first few cycles how much you can expect to be accomplished and how that relates to how much performance was expected in the past—the origin of the present corporate performance (or nonperformance) culture.

As a note, by "cycles," I do not mean set periods of a certain number of days. These cycles will not necessarily take up the same amount of time unless you intentionally plan for the strategic management process to be an institutionalized, calendar-based engagement. A "cycle" signifies completing and reinitiating the strategic management process. It can refer to all three individual practices or the trinity itself as a whole. For instance, if your organization's strategic thinking is ongoing, with some specific work being completed at specific times of the year, then the practice is both active and passive. The active portions may be equally spaced throughout the calendar year, and their completion and particular output signals may initiate the strategy development practice. If the current strategy is amplified by the ongoing environmental changes (internal and external) that the team has identified, then the strategic planning process may be very minimal and nuanced. Perhaps the team will suggest that many of the objectives remain in play and performance expectations increase to a specified level—to keep the performance culture engaged. Of course, the actual planning process is not passive. It takes place at a set time during the year. The overarching organizational strategic goals are not changed often, as that would diminish the value of insights gathered and decided upon in the strategy development work. In faster paced industries, however, the length of a strategic planning process and the longevity of the plans created will differ. Yours should match the health care industry, and you will understand the speed of change by monitoring the environmental forces. Be aware, however, that depending on your market, your competitors may be lax to change for significant improvement until forced. In that instance, remember the need for innovation and the clarion call for it across industries for the sake of stakeholders' benefit. Do not let the laggards and the value-slackers be your benchmark. Your mission is too important.

Defined Responsibility

Responsibility is a linchpin factor of execution. If someone is responsible for a task, then to the degree the task is significant to the organizational mission and the individual is concerned both for the organizational mission and their role in the organization, it is more likely to be accomplished.

At the same time, we need responsibility expectations to be commensurate with the authority individuals and units have. But when it comes to high-performance organizations that consistently act strategically, openness and horizontal structures of authority can be quite helpful. Such structuring enables wide application of responsibility, rather than bottlenecking highly important actions and activities with individuals who are likely to have several other mission critical responsibilities. Navigating this dilemma is less about limiting the kinds of actions and activities that flow up (vertical hierarchy) and instead focusing long term on raising competencies of workers so that decision making capacity across the organization rises. Tools such as responsibility assignment matrices (RACI) may prove useful here.

Identified Constraints

Key to your execution of strategic plans will be the access to and availability of necessary resources when the time calls for them. Time, personnel, cash, relationships—these are all resources and potential constraints on objective accomplishment. People get sick or depart the organization for reasons you cannot necessarily understand or control. Important relationships get severed through mismanagement and misbehavior. Investment values rise and fall, suppliers go out of business, insurance claims are filed but require processing periods, and important documents go missing. All sorts of issues can derail your scheduled sequence of important actions and activities. These need to be identified to some degree in your plans. You might mark potential volatility within the plan and note different decision pathways for those of the most significant concern given their mission criticalness. Certainly, your planning cannot provide for every contingency, but it would be wise to plan for some, or to plan generally with allotments of additional buffer time for overall completion. I use time as the medium of contingency since with more time you can generally find alternative means for accessing key resources. Though we do not want to unintentionally delay execution with such allowances.

Unit leaders are often in a difficult position of wanting to have the right amount of time for team members to complete time-intensive work while also encouraging performance improvement in the form of speed and quality. These seem mutually exclusive desires. Thus, one way to encourage the allowance for buffers within the sequencing is to reward units according to unused buffer time. Having the responsibility to achieve is tethered to the reward for the kind of achievement the organization desires. Simultaneously, the unit should also be given the authority to make adjustments for both accomplishment and improvement. To do this right, you would first need to ensure the reward is equitable according to who carries the greatest burden within a task sequence. They are the individuals for whom the time is most necessary, and therefore most valuable. In one measure, their task and their approach to accomplishing it efficiently (with regard to time use) is a constraint upon objective completion. Your aim should be to motivate their task completion through external rewards and intrinsic value encouragement. The former can be accomplished more generally, with regard to all teams, but the latter will need to be more personalized and understood through relationships formed with those critical individuals. You can look for ways to tie their personal motivations to the organization's mission, which can help drive task accomplishment, but you will also need to be mindful of whether the individual has bought into the organization's mission—or if they are capable of doing so. While many people are highly competent, if they are not of the same character as the organization requires, which includes a concern for others over their selves as a display of cultural strength, then they are more of a liability than an asset. Individuals who are unwilling to attempt and promote performance improvement need to find another home base for their abilities, as more time seldom persuades. Our organizations can no longer remain stagnant and smile about it. We need people intensely focused on providing better care for our patients and carrying each other along the way as we grow at different paces—the key being growth.

Intended Measurability

Finally, the plan must address actions and activities in measurable terms. By this, I mean the plan must have quantitative expectations against which you and the unit leaders can take "snapshots" of the levels at which their units are performing in given criteria, and then those snapshots can be measured against the sequenced expectations on the strategic plan.

The idea here is that comparison requires equivalence in terms. If apples and oranges are incomparable overall, then we need to ensure all our fruit are understood in more comparable terms (acidity, texture, water content, and so on). Additionally—and this is vitally important—unmet or superseded expectations can only be identified because of previous forecasts, which may have been developed during the strategic thinking foresight exercises. Remember, foresight is not simply about prediction and accuracy. Those are not unimportant aspects, but they are subservient to and far less important than foresight's assumption—expansion work on the whole. In the case of measurability, however, forecasting accuracy does have its place to shine. Its importance relates to its signaling effect that can help improve the entire strategic management process.

Your initial foresight work was a structure of assumptions by which you could have projected certain accomplishments among units. If those forecasted expectations were met, then you might make the case that either your interpretation of the environment's changes was correct (assuming you followed your strategic plan closely and it logically followed from the input–foresight–output process) or that the environmental shifts and execution of the strategic plan were changed at proportional rates and therefore produced analogous outcomes. In my experience, in environments of great unpredictability and radical change, we are more likely to experience greater than or less than performances (exception: if you have the capacity to change inputs and execution when approaching the expected outcomes and so purposefully limit output). Either preproduction ramps up to meet demand or plants are shuttered early to avoid earned failures. In such environments, forecasts can provide much more important signaling. The signal that we produced more than is regularly sustainable or less than we expected and need is incredibly valuable. Obviously, such signals announce we failed to meet expectations, and if efforts and attitudes to accomplish tasks and the mission were no more or less than in previous periods of evaluation, then it can also be assumed that either the foresight or strategy development was flawed. In the case of flawed strategy development, we simply did not connect the best possible strategies with foreseen expectations, as if we knew there was a turn coming up, but we drove by thinking a roundabout route would be more expedient. In the case of flawed foresight, we did not even know about the turn. As you can see, quality foresight gives us more options, but it does not keep us from making mistakes. Having measurable terms in our strategic plans, therefore, can help us improve both our foresight work of interpreting the changing world around us and also our strategy development work of applying strategic decision making according to those interpretations.

Summary

You need to exercise strategic thinking, strategy development, and strategic planning in your organization for a single reason: that your stakeholders win their game. These three practices, a trinity of varied efforts to accomplish the unified purpose of strategically managing the organization, are often confused and misrepresented as competitors rather than as complementary actors. As management strategy expert Henry Mintzberg (1994) writes,

> When companies understand the difference between planning and strategic thinking, they can get back to what the strategy-making process should be: capturing what the manager learns from all sources [both the soft insights from his or her own personal experiences and the experiences of others throughout the organization and the hard data from market research and the like] and then synthesizing that learning into a vision of the direction that the business should pursue.[12]

Though Mintzberg did not address strategy development as I have above, his point here is in agreement. Unlike strategic planning, strategic thinking is an ongoing behavior for approaching situations, involving the aggregation of any and all information available, assuming all is potentially relevant to the circumstances for which such thinking is put to work. In contrast, strategy development focuses like a laser on the outputs from such thinking, which seem significant because of the pre-work. Then, planning, like a congealing substance, gives us confidence to execute on

---

[12] Mintzberg, H. 1994. "The Fall and Rise of Strategic Planning." *Harvard Business Review* 72, no. 1, 107–114. *Business Source Complete,* EBSCO*host* (accessed on June 9, 2015).

our assumptions with well-defined actions and activities in real time, for the sake of improving our organization's standing. Why is it that around 70 percent of strategies fail to be executed properly?[13] Perhaps it has to do with the disintegration of ties between these disciplines.

Too many believe in some irreconcilable animosity between planning and thinking (which they align with creativity). They argue that planning tends to rely on past performance to determine future performance as well as assumes regularity in situation conditions and other parties' behaviors, whereas strategic thinking keeps an open eye, expecting change and preparing to synthesize it with what is already known. To some degree this is true, but it does not speak to their compatibility. If we may only plan once and never change, then planning is incredibly weak—even more than we have been told; but, that is not a scenario we often face. We are often capable of learning and incorporating that learning within a period of time during which we are still doing the same kinds of activities. Advocates for strategic thinking should not deny it, unless they want to upend the premise of strategic thinking, for they consider it continually creative as an approach to interpreting situations, allowing for and benefiting from multiple perspectives, *utilizing* insights pertaining to the subtle and nuanced as well as the extremely dynamic and groundbreaking. With these, foresight becomes possible. Additionally, the past is not discarded, since it is a valuable source of information; instead, it enriches the picture painted by the present situational realities and future probabilities. Some may desire to simply think creatively, but our health care organizations need action. We need solutions. We need to test our insights and improve our outcomes. The only way to meet that intention is to fuse their practices into the strategic management process, where planning engages our assumptions, projections, and decisions with real-time activities, forcing us to get serious about leveraging our strategic minds. We need strategic mindfulness that does not simply play, it performs. To ensure that, we will now consider the craft each of us is called to cultivate: leadership.

---

[13] Kaplan, R., and D. Norton. 2009. *The Strategy-Focused Organization: How Balanced Scorecard Companies Thrive in the New Business Environment*, 1–3. Boston, MA: Harvard Business School Press.

CHAPTER 4

Integrative Leadership

To reduce confusion, the foundational notion of leadership itself is taken herein as, "a process whereby an individual influences a group of individuals to achieve a common goal."[1] What we know about leadership is what it does, which gives us insight into what it is. In this sense, we can know leadership analogously. This is one reason why this book conjures the understanding that innovation, strategy, and leadership exist as an integrative process. As we covered how the decriers of strategic planning rightly grasp the scientific limitations of static information, interpretations, and choices to offer flexibility and resiliency, so too does a view of leadership limited to strengths and weaknesses, personalities and prerogatives, or any other number of attributes truncate its available power. Numerous specialized conceptualizations of leadership have arisen over the years, some better documented and researched than others, but all with their intention to crack parts of this process's code. Among all these approaches to the field, there are three practices that, though they do not comprise all there is to leadership, are most suitable for inclusion in a discussion about innovating leadership: anticipatory leadership (forward looking), strategic leadership (laterally aware and proactive), and administrative leadership (consciously efficient).

Leadership and Innovation Kiss

Given the discussion of innovation in Chapter 2, the key frames to which our leadership question needs to be applied are the context of innovation, effectiveness in innovating, and the sustenance of innovativeness. In other words, these forms of leadership address:

---

[1] Northouse, P.G. 2013. *Leadership: Theory and Practice,* 5, 6th ed. Thousand Oaks, CA: Sage Publications, Inc.

1. Where is or might innovation be coming from? → Anticipation
2. How should innovation look in our context? → Strategy
3. How can innovativeness be maintained? → Administration

Even more simply, one might see these as the three domains of external inquiry and internal effectiveness in our first actions and efficiency in subsequent actions. Often, proponents of touted leadership approaches seclude themselves within the confines of their "theory," which is severely inhibitive for organizational leaders. Leaders need the flexibility to say, "This theory isn't working here; I need to try something else." Nevertheless, they can only make such statements confidently and experience minimal constraint if saying that is not the same in their own minds as "This theory doesn't work. I need to try something else." The key difference is the context: *here*. Circumstances, being ever changing, ensure that no leader ever faces the same situation with exactly the same particulars— just like the proverbial man never enters the same river twice, for just as the water changes, so also he is a different man each time.

That issue of context, then, is what can make or break a theory of leadership's application. Surely, you might want to offer some pushback on this point. However, if you were to do so, then it would be a result of assumptions most leadership approaches already take for granted, like whether the theory in use in your organizational paradigm is assumed to be universally applicable, contextual, or cultural. In your health care organization, you will likely find some leadership models work to promote positive change better than others. You will likely find that some describe your successes and failures better, while others describe attitudes and behaviors better. Some will have great academic and industry research behind them but seem altogether foreign to your industry or organizational profile. The dissonance could be your chaotic mess of an organization, but it would be best to remember that models are like metaphors, and they breakdown in application when used incessantly and generally.

Nevertheless, some clear assumptions that do not conflict with the three forms (anticipatory, strategic, administrative) need to be agreed upon as leadership essentials. That is to say, there are some aspects to leadership that—at least in the global west—are foundationally important for the leadership process to achieve its potential. Those aspects are neatly addressed by leadership researchers Kouzes and Posner in their perennially acclaimed book, *The Leadership Challenge*, in which they point out that the core of the leadership process runs on the fuel of credibility, without which the rest of the endeavor eventually, in the best case, falls into disrepair. Upon that bedrock of trust, where leaders and the individuals they influence share a paradigm that what each says and does is nestled in mutual faithfulness, Kouzes and Posner introduced what they called the Five Practices:

1. "Model the Way.
2. Inspire a Shared Vision.
3. Challenge the Process.
4. Enable Others to Act.
5. Encourage the Heart."[2]

In short, these are often the unexpressed, sine qua non's of leadership influence. Each has its own colloquial proverbs most are familiar with—except that Kouzes and Posner did the legwork and have the data to argue their findings. For instance, the first deals with setting the example for followers to imitate. If leaders do not want followers to do something (due to organizational values concerns), then, at the least, the leaders should not do it themselves. The second pertains to hope, and that followers want to think of themselves and their work as significant. Such is entirely natural and accomplishable if your work and organization is tied to an end morally superior to financial statements, and sharing that hope vital. Within the health care context, this has traditionally been a practice that engaged almost no opposition. Today, however, tight budgets, questionable nonprofit statuses forcing regulatory changes, for-profit distinctions, and a slew of other issues has caused some practitioners to lose their inspiration. Be aware of how deep the rumors run around you.

Kouzes and Posner's notion of change comes third, which they understand as being a combination of continual learning and early adoption. This practice undergirds what will be addressed in the next chapter,

---

[2] Kouzes, J.M., and B.Z. Posner. 2002. *The Leadership Challenge*, 13, 3rd ed. San Francisco: Jossey-Bass.

especially in regard to anticipatory foresight practices. Essentially, following the first practice, they argue for leaders to illustrate the adoption of new ideas and methods before expecting their followers do. The fourth practice follows this lead, in part by the fact that followers' trust for their leaders and their organizational visions grows through the modeling they witness. Likewise, being included in the leaders' work and engaging in the same kind of practices helps create a safe environment for testing organizational norms and cultural habits in order to achieve the inspiring vision—which is elevated in organizational importance above mere form and function. Simply, if the leader does it, then others *can* do it, since the end game is mission accomplished. If the leader is engaging the five practices when this happens, then the followers' behaviors would likely be impossible to condemn. Finally, Kouzes and Posner highlight the critical importance of the interpersonal side of relationship building to the leadership process. By modeling their values through encouraging their followers, whether with rewards and appreciation or otherwise, leaders are crafting space for higher yields of intraorganizational trust. Where people are well treated and cared for, trust is protected along with the organization's unity—both of which are essential for achieving long-term goals.

Immediately upon looking at Kouzes and Posner's data from a questionnaire on "Characteristics of Admired Leaders," one notices the top four are significantly better rated by respondents—and have continued to be since the first edition of the questionnaire was issued in 1987.[3] The authors note this consistent admiration is not only across time, but also across the globe, as it was administered in Australia, Canada, Japan, Korea, Malaysia, Mexico, New Zealand, Scandinavia, Singapore, and the United States to over 75,000 individuals. These four characteristics, in descending order from most admired are: honest, forward-looking, competent, and inspiring. Each of these not only undergird the Five Practices, but they also tie in well with the more specific leadership practices (anticipatory, strategic, and administrative) mentioned previously.

To begin, *anticipatory leadership* is the epitome of forward-looking inspiration, being the kind of leadership that is hyper-sensitive to the external environment, rarely surprised by peripheral shifts in industries

---

[3] Kouzes, J.M., and B.Z. Posner. 2002. *The Leadership Challenge*, 24–25, 3rd ed. San Francisco: Jossey-Bass.

and society because it never stagnates in the present-past plateau. Through foresight, this leadership inspires with visionary imagining couched in a comprehensive knowledge of the macro-environment. Next, *strategic leadership* is where the forward-looking nature of leadership merges with the honesty of what is critical to success. Such leadership can understand the intersections of an anticipated reality, desired vision, and experience. It neither discounts the future for the sake of the past nor falsifies the difficulties experienced to reach the present. Lastly, *administrative leadership* is the response to irreproachable honesty on current conditions and competencies. With such faithful inventories, it focuses on accomplishing the long-term building effort, ensuring efficiency and reliability of the output. In short, anticipatory leadership identifies the future to which the present needs to bridge, strategic leadership notes where that bridge needs to be located and the project's critical necessities, and administrative leadership oversees the effort to a completion that engenders further opportunities than initially envisioned. When leveraged together, these three practices of leadership produce a sum greater than its parts, an *integrative leadership model* primed to help your organization generate outstanding healthcare outcomes of the innovation kind.

Strategic Choice

To understand why integrative leadership is so important, we need to understand the key models it is based on. This starts with strategic choice. At its core, this concept relates to organizations aligning with their environments and advocates against the notion that firms are the pawns of their environmental monarchs. Leaders' decisions have significant impact on how their organizations are structured and perform. Even more, the notion suggests they have the capacity to contextually terraform, that is, actually change the environment to some degree rather than only adapting to it. The most persuasive and helpful work I have found in this regard comes from business professors Raymond Miles and Charles Snow, whose version of strategic choice breaks down into five areas of consideration:

1. *Dominant Coalition*: There are chief decision makers who find and solve key issues.

2. *Perceptions*: The dominant coalition defines the organization's paradigm. What they see as important is managed, and everyone sees it. What they ignore rarely enters the decision making agenda.

3. *Segmentation*: The dominant coalition must determine how divisible the operational environment is, rank it by importance, and establish responsibility and resource allocation to lesser coalitions for their management.

4. *Scanning Activities*: The dominant coalition must monitor critical organizational issues within their operating environment and respond to them or preempt action.

5. *Dynamic Constraints*: The dominant coalition, constrained by past decisions, can adjust their decisions, accepting that changes will generate new constraints.[4]

Essentially, this approach argues that we shape our environments with the strategies *we choose* to employ; meaning, as leaders, we affect the way we perceive the environment. At the same time, to argue that we have the capacity to shape our environment suggests we are an, "active player in creating opportunities and/or threats."[5] In that respect, our health care environments operate according to the laws of quantum physics, where our observation and interaction with our market space also necessarily changes it. If our strategy is one of defending market share and client relationships, then our environmental perception will be different from the organization embarking on a path to disrupt the current market and/ or develop a new market. In a systems sense, this approach illustrates how resilient systems are to change; but, at the same time these systems' resiliency comes from two places: (1) using slack to endure high pressure fluctuations and (2) evolving new responses to balance the system when pressure exceeds capacity. Some systems collapse under excessive pressure, but since the systems we are envisioning are markets of people,

---

[4] Miles, R.E., and C.C. Snow. 2003. *Organizational Strategy, Structure, and Process*, 20–21. Stanford, CA: Stanford University Press.

[5] Dent, E.B. 1999. "Complexity Science: A Worldview Shift." *Emergence* 1, no. 4, no. 5. Business Source Complete, EBSCOhost. (accessed on March 3, 2019)

these systems necessarily adapt. Why? We have an incentive through self-interest to supply the market fix; and, we have the capabilities with innovation to change the system for higher load capacity. As the earlier discussion should have made clear, either the innovation will add additional support for the current structure of the market (sustaining innovations), or it might change the shape of the system entirely in order to dramatically improve the system's operation without requiring significantly more resources (disruptive innovation). How does this happen? The answer is through the *adaptive cycle*, the application of the insight that organization design and structure follows the strategies we select.

The Adaptive Cycle

The adaptive cycle, the first model of note that gives credibility to the integrative delivery solution, concerns the three primary issues an organization has an ongoing need to settle throughout the course of its existence. These are issues that provide a unified perspective for the organization, the leaders within, and the environment without. Health care organizations are not outliers, but they must also answer the questions to these problems on a repeated basis, and those answers—encapsulated in their strategic management process—determine success and failure. Miles and Snow label these:

- *The Entrepreneurial Problem*[6]—Organizations come into existence when they can define their entrepreneurial insight in the form of an organizational domain, for example, we make clinical needles type 1 or provide needle disposal service 2 for target market of X-sized outpatient clinics or market segment of patients allergic to metallic needles.
- *The Engineering Problem*—With each proposed entrepreneurial solution that the organization pursues, there comes a need to establish a system that can accomplish it, for example, Units 1 and 2 provide real-time surgery decision support through

---

[6] Miles, R.E., and C.C. Snow. 2003. *Organizational Strategy, Structure, and Process*, 21–22. Stanford, CA: Stanford University Press.

broadband videoconferencing and telecommunications
technologies for clinicians operating in quarantine zones, etc.

- *The Administrative Problem*—While the system solutions for
  the engineering problem bring the entrepreneurial insight
  to life, the uncertainty that comes with it needs mitigation.
  This occurs as the system's activities are stabilized. Moreover,
  with the added stability comes a reduction in resource
  requirements and an increase in the opportunities to develop
  additional support systems for entrepreneurial insight
  development. Examples of such solutions include monitoring
  systems for product output and performance evaluation, such
  as of turnover rates or patient satisfaction by unit, length
  of stay, product profitability, R & D expenses and general
  budgeting, etc.

Thus, the cycle originally "starts" with the entrepreneurial problem
requiring a solution. That threshold being met signals the need for an
engineering problem solution. Within competitive environments, those
solutions provide the spark for initiation but not sustainability, which is
where the administrative solutions emerge. Then, either because the original insight is too early for majority adoption, narrow in its market appeal,
weak in its comparative offering, or costly in its resource use, organizations need to generate additional or alternative entrepreneurial insights.
These may arise alongside the original insight, after a period of the original insight's decline in relevance, or simply because the organization finds
itself with additional capacity. The organization, therefore, reengages the
primary problems with new and/or hybrid solutions. In a sense, cycles of
cycles emerge over time.

Of key importance in this model is that the administrative solution is
both freeing and constraining for the organization. What I mean by that
is the administrative solutions create organizational slack. They help you
become more efficient and reduce your uncertainty with the aid of systems and processes that reduce resource consumption (especially time).
But, with that addition comes a constraint in the form of less flexibility.
How? When structures and processes are established to increase the efficiency of a product/service or production/delivery activity, they naturally

confine operations. That constrains future actions and the capacity to shift should circumstances change and unfavorably affect the present structures and processes. For instance, and I am sure this is an example needing little introduction, consider software upgrades or conversions to new platforms. They often come as a means to (re)deliver greater value on the entrepreneurial and engineering problems, but prior administrative solutions increase the difficulty of their implementation. That is to say that prior administrative solutions, which increased efficiency at the time, regularly increase the difficulty later experienced in implementing new solutions.

A similar dilemma is often displayed through product delivery chain and value-chain strategies. Making this vividly clear is the question of vertical integration. To vertically integrate would entail bringing as many sourcing, production, and delivery activities in-house as possible and profitable (upstream and downstream). Often, this strategy is resource-intensive, but it provides an additional level of both control over your market system and resiliency against supplier, purchaser, and delivery constraints. In contrast, sourcing beyond your organization can reduce costs by leaving particular activities to organizations with scale or scope advantages (groups that only focus on X-surgeries or networks that provide a plethora of insurance plans). These examples have hopefully shown you that administrative solutions bring clear structure to engineering solutions, meaning they show up late in the process because of the time it takes to adjust for efficiency. With that being true, however, comes the question of how to limit the constraining force of administrative solutions. How do you both gain value through efficiency while also not freeze out your future prospects? One solution would be the development of divergent systems or organizational units whose single aim is to horizontally integrate experience and learning within their domain. Another would be to outsource solutions constrained by the more strategically important ones which need to remain in-house in order to sustain competitive advantage.

If the answer is so clear in how adaptation occurs, then we must ask why organizations, including our own, seem to find adapting so often difficult. This proves to be a question of execution, not just of executing strategies and plans, but of executing leadership practices. For instance, we might argue that shortsighted rather than foresighted thinking limits many leaders' capacity to *see* the need for adapting when it arises. We might similarly suggest that leaders lack the leadership competencies to act appropriately: to perceive, decide, and administrate in accordance with the situation's demands. Moreover, leaders, being self-interested to some degree, may be inhibited by the probabilities that particular decisions would impinge on their personal expectations. Doing right by the organization might appear to impose on their "rights." Just consider the health care worker who is entitled to particular benefits, and remains in the organization though wanting to exit in order to dip into those perks. Surely, the problem could be the calcification of the organization's adaptive cycle, but that too would only be a constraint imposed by the decisions of past leaders. Ultimately, leadership demands a higher level of integrity to make selfless decisions. It costs you—or it costs them.

The Flexible Leadership Model

Continuing in this theme for models that integrate rather than separate, we need to look at the flexible leadership model of Gary Yukl and Richard Lepsinger. It arose from the two researchers' interest in developing a model for leadership effectiveness. The problem they faced was that most of the research and conclusions available seemed inconclusive and unproductive. Essentially, their own research over the decades had given them pause about the efficacy of leadership studies. They write:

> Having a better way to view leadership behavior was not sufficient to explain how leaders can affect organization performance. Two more things were needed to clarify this connection. First, it was necessary to understand the internal processes and external events that determine whether an organization will survive and prosper. Second, it was necessary to understand how leaders are able to influence these processes in a significant way.[7]

These realizations led them to draft assumptions about the relationships between efficiency, adaptation, and human relations, organizational

---

[7] Yukl, G., and R. Lepsinger. 2004. *Flexible Leadership: Creating Value by Balancing Multiple Challenges and Choices,* 21. San Francisco: Jossey-Bass.

environments, and leadership influence, which they tested to discover the model. Basically, their model tries to frame out how effective leaders know what to do, how to do, and when to do so much better than others, eventually asserting that high-performance leadership, "is a response to continually changing situations, that leaders need to find an appropriate balance among competing demands, and that leadership must be coordinated and consistent across levels and subunits."[8] As you might recognize, this model seems like it should align well with the strategic-choice perspective because of its emphasis on adaptation and environmental change awareness. Furthermore, the continued focus on effectiveness is highlighted in the flexible leadership model more than in other models because of its focus on behavior. *It is a model that lets actions rather than ideas tell most of the story about how leadership that improves organizational performance actually works.* More regarding the specifics of their flexible leadership model will show up in later chapters, where portions of it and its theoretical underpinnings align with administrative leadership.

Robert Keidel's Triadic Model

Robert Keidel's triadic model is our third waypoint on this journey for organizational leadership insight. Keidel's starting point is that "We make decisions based on the way we frame life. We decide—and design—as we think (and feel). In other words, human organization reflects cognitive organization."[9] He lays out his model, arguing it is rooted in how humans engage in peaceful relationships, with the format of a triangle, where relationships are determined by how two parties engage one another. Fundamentally, they can either make decisions together, make decisions separately, or one can make decisions for them both. Keidel identifies these means of relationship as cooperation, autonomy, and control respectively. In one sense, therefore, this model of human relationships is also a model of organizational design potential, since organizations are

---

[8] Yukl, G., and R. Lepsinger. 2004. *Flexible Leadership: Creating Value by Balancing Multiple Challenges and Choices,* 19–23. San Francisco: Jossey-Bass.
[9] Keidel, R. 1995. *Seeing Organizational Patterns: A New Theory and Language of Organization Design,* 5. San Francisco: Berrett-Koehler Publishers Inc.

conglomerations of human relationships. Of course, they can become more complex through mixtures of each, and the integration of technology furthers the organizational structure complexity.

As it regards how this model also relates to strategy, consider this: Strategy aligns with intent, and structure aligns with action. Where this puts our discussion so far, then, is that we and our organizations routinely face changing environments. These dynamic shifts calls for differing strategies, because our intentions change as the environment inhibits and allows for certain effectiveness with our present playbooks. Changes to plans can be costly and are certainly frustrating when they appear outside of our control. Thus, we need some kind of paradigm that permits alignment in the form of strategy-integration. Keidel's model presents such an option, because it relates our capacity for strategic action to our structures for relating. For instance, organizational units that function without much dependency on others and are not required to check with particular leaders in order to engage in their primary service activity could be said to have autonomy-based design. This kind of design is frequently employed by organizations with global offices where cultural and regulatory differences force the organization to behave dramatically different in diverse regions. In one respect, the organization trades the control value of efficiency and the cooperation value of intention for the autonomy value of effectiveness. The international unit is given the freedom to operate in a way that "works" in that context rather than forcing it to follow the routine disciplined methods and policies that may or may not fit the home office's context either! Because, in this example, the company's highest priority is effectiveness in the operational environment, they are also less concerned about increasing constraints that forced-sharing might incur—even though it could improve understanding and future flexibility if the context changes. Of course, the other means are not truly absent; they are simply diminished in light of the more prioritized means of relating at that organizational decision point.

With a mixture of structures, then, we have the potential to rapidly shift our strategic efforts—at least in comparison to relatively fixed, uniformly enforced, organizational structures. For example, complete hierarchies may be capable of gaining efficiencies through policy and protocol, but such rigidity is rarely safe. Such one-sided approaches (like the former example of hierarchy/control) to organizational structure are increasingly susceptible to failure, highlighting the value of the triadic model. The hierarchical organization misses out on huge gains from the other forms of relating. Consider autonomy once more, for management literature is rife with examples and conclusions explaining the value that can accrue from employee independence. For example, one set of experts argue that,

> Management should encourage their employees to think independently and should provide them with the freedom to respond to work situations and problems, so that they are able to satisfy the idiosyncratic needs and requests of the many and heterogeneous customers. When employees are given more autonomy, their sense of responsibility to the organization is bound to increase, and correspondingly, they become more accountable for actions in their jobs.[10]

They also point out how important autonomy can be for creating safe organizational space. You have likely heard of the notion that having a "freedom to fail" usually precedes the understanding that you have the freedom to succeed, because most organizational cultures have promoted the control variable. That control variable leads to safety-promoting behavior. Failing to deliver when experimenting for the sake of innovation is inherently fear-inducing in such environments, and so it tends to be avoided. Of course, overreliance on autonomy will naturally backfire and hinder organizational unity, integration of new and successful developments, and the efficiency gains reaped in controlled institutionalization of best practices. For instance, interacting spontaneously, behavior highly promoted among the organizations that led the transformation to the digital age, generated powerful synergies. However, that same commitment *also* made it vastly more difficult to parse out the credit for innovations

---

[10] Sousa, C.M.P., F. Coelho, and E. Guillamon-Saorin. 2012. "Personal Values, Autonomy, and Self-Efficacy: Evidence from Frontline Service Employees." *International Journal of Selection and Assessment* 20, no. 2, 159–170. Academic Search Alumni Edition, EBSCOhost (accessed on July 1, 2015).

that took place during the same period.[11] Additionally, under-reliance on one of the three means of relating is similarly dangerous, and assuming one can organize without priority (meaning entirely equal emphases on each) will certainly inhibit the organization's prospects.[12] Why? The means exist to provide organizations with the resiliency to relate on a need-to basis given their environmental contexts.

The problem with alignment and integration of conflicting means is that reducing conflict between the means also reduces their power to deliver on their priorities. For control, the prioritization is efficiency. To reduce control for the sake of gaining collaboration (prioritizing relationships most conducive to flexibility and innovation) would also require a reduction in the efficiency of the organization at that point. Costs will increase. Actions will be less structured and codified, and there may be conflict because hierarchies are not in place where one party's voice determines whether another party's voice is heard. Yes, strangely, adding the element of cooperation has the likelihood of promoting conflict in what were heavily control-oriented organizations prior to the shift. Such trade-offs actually exist across the entire triadic model, and helping reveal this is one of the model's strongest and most insightful powers.

As health care organization leaders, understanding how such blending of divergent priorities occurs and enhances our organizations' capacity to adapt and lead in complex and seemingly chaotic environments can make for an invaluable competitive advantage. For example, consider what it would look like to apply the triadic model to information flow. At the surface level, information can flow by the three means of relating upward, downward, and laterally. When information flows up the organizational leadership chain, the work of autonomous relating is occurring. Lower-ranked individuals do not pass information upward in control and collaborative environments. Many understand why the former is true but not the latter. Let me explain, in collaborative environments we share information with our peers, but we still have a sense of confinement

---

[11] Isaacson, W. 2014. *The Innovators: How a Group of Hackers, Geniuses, and Geeks Created the Digital Revolution.* New York, NY: Simon and Schuster.

[12] Keidel, R. 1995. *Seeing Organizational Patterns: A New Theory and Language of Organization Design.* San Francisco: Berrett-Koehler Publishers Inc.

within a structure. This presence of mind is what allows us to recognize others as peers and respect the relationship as something collaborative. In contrast, autonomy enables free decision making, the kind that makes someone feel comfortable sending a complaint or recommendation to another individual who is many years their senior in experience and many levels their rank without some explicit relationship or authorization. These means of relating are not good or bad in themselves, but depending on how structures are deployed to emphasize one means over another, your units will face communication friction, have more or less capability to implement strategic changes, require uniform behavior, and so on. In that sense, your structural changes force trade-offs in structural power. Being *aware* of this, coupled with our strategic intentions, is vital. As Keidel tell us, "unless an organization periodically thinks through issues of constituencies, character, and capabilities—why we exist, what we are, and how we satisfy customers—the odds are strong that it will lose direction and founder, no matter how rigorously it addresses matters of structure and systems."[13] In essence, that is organizational strategy.

One concept that should immediately become clear is that your entire organization does not and should not necessarily be uniformly run according to the same pattern for relating. Your finance department might require significant structures for control, but emergency surgery teams might call for significant collaborative-adaptive structures instead. Would it not be horrific to find out a surgery failed because control structures hindered valuable opportunities for team members to provide life-saving suggestions and act immediately according to their expertise rather than wait for a controlling policy and hierarchy to give them allowance? In the same way, are we not regularly bombarded with glowing service-oriented testimonies that argue how sales and customer service teams that are empowered to operate autonomously are empowered to serve stakeholders in creative and meaningful ways? This triadic model gives one of the critical solutions to our dilemma of having structure follow strategy, and yet needing different kinds of structures to fully empower the diverse strategy landscape.

---

[13] Keidel, R. 1995. *Seeing Organizational Patterns: A New Theory and Language of Organization Design,* 63. San Francisco: Berrett-Koehler Publishers Inc.

At this point, you should grasp why you need to understand this and the preceding models: Competitive advantages quickly speed away in today's markets, making the discovery or creation of an internal mechanism that can sustain competitive advantage your chief work. Patterns and paradigms enter the mix as a *means* for a strategic thinker like yourself to evaluate the internal and external contexts for design. In this way, patterns are frameworks for thinking and they generate efficiency in the strategic thinking process. Keidel's use of triangles illustrates the organizing principle of human relationships to bring a greater whole out of the parts. In identifying that organizational complexity can be simplified, he presents a vision for sustainable competitive advantage through unique prioritization, integration, and focus:

1. Prioritize among the three means to ensure trade-offs give you strength where you believe the organization needs it most (like cost/control, differentiation/autonomy, or flexibility/cooperation);
2. Integrate the chosen levels of all three primary means of relating as each is essential to organizational longevity; and
3. Keep attentive to the environmental shifts and which variable is most affected. This kind of strategic choice cannot be easily imitated.

In today's environment, this triadic model seems to point in the same direction Keidel emphasized as gaining ascendancy twenty years ago, toward the dominance of an autonomy—cooperation hybrid. On the one hand, newness is prized, and on the other, integration is. In regard to our focus on how does a health care organization deliver innovation sustainably (not to be confused with sustaining innovation), we should be able to quickly realize that autonomy promotes personal creative freedom and self-control, whereas cooperation promotes collaborative environments in which innovations can disseminate throughout the organization effectively. In the long run, organizations that innovate at the fringes without integrating their developments will fracture. These cases may lead to spin-offs, and in many industrial settings that solution works well, allowing specified focus and distinctive competency buildup. In health care, however, the greater sector need is for integrated innovations.

You are keenly aware of the troubles faced with electronic medical records and the portability of information across providers and payers and everyone else who makes a case for needing the information. Even in-house we find the sharing of information difficult and a cause of myriad delays.

The triadic framework needs no further explanation, though I highly encourage reading Keidel's work for your own enrichment. For our purposes herein, however, the key takeaway from the triadic model is recognizing how integrative it is across organizational activities and purposes and also how well the triadic model interprets highly divergent contexts. Along with the other models previously discussed, the triadic model presents a framework for understanding organization design, environmental flux, and leadership variables. Together, these theoretical structures support the integrative leadership model.

Delivering an Integrative Trinity of Leadership Practices

Earlier I mentioned the three practices of leadership that comprise the integrative leadership model. These are anticipatory leadership, strategic leadership, and administrative leadership. In the following three chapters we will look at each leadership practice in greater detail to understand its makeup and purpose. From the models already presented, it should become increasingly clear how the integrative leadership model builds on the findings and experiences of decades of strategic management, organization design, and leadership research. From the get-go, you should recognize that the adaptive cycle covers the questions which each leadership practice will address in turn. The entrepreneurial problem is handled by anticipatory leadership, the engineering problem with strategic leadership, and the administrative problem with administrative leadership. This model permits leaders to be interested and invested in innovation development processes, that is, effectively and efficiently sustaining the present with a goal to actively and positively shape the future.

Regarding the seeming choices organizational leaders face, I do not agree that efficiency and effectiveness goals are ultimately opposed. In the daily choices for building systems, we promote both. Efficiency gains last only as long as the solution they promote remains a market winner and further efficiency cannot be extracted. Likewise, effective solutions lose their marginal gains over time in markets where the onset of innovation increases the options available and preferences that providers can satisfy. For instance, when providers could only remedy an acute condition and could not (or did not think to) offer end-to-end service, the desire for a one-stop medical journey could never be preferred by patients over other options. Now that patients have the growing option for such care, other providers have to take notice and consider the competitive effectiveness of their offerings. Furthermore, the integrative leadership model certainly aligns with the triadic model's organization of complexity into the simplicity of three forms of interaction. Each of the leadership practices falls neatly into focus with autonomy, cooperation, and control. And, like the model provides, each practice can further be considered as a balancing act of the three variables in its own right.

Summary

Significant differences remain between the former leadership models and what you find within the practices of the integrative leadership model. One difference is apparent in how the models deal with description and prescription and the degree to which they do so. In large part, the previous models engage in both. They may explain and interpret the environment in which your organization competes, or they might explain and interpret your organization itself, and how it operates. Among these, the flexible leadership model also engages in the most prescription, as it focuses on effective behaviors that create value. The adaptive cycle also prescribes organizational pathways to some degree, though the dynamism of current market circumstances and ongoing organizational activities are sometimes difficult to combine with the sector-competitive view that it deals with. The integrative leadership model, however, takes the insights from these models and prescribes the activities each leadership practice expertly trains in to accomplish its legitimate end.

To be abundantly clear, the integrative leadership model aims to incorporate the realization that health care desperately needs innovation (and it needs it to be done well) with support from the best solutions of strategic management and leadership research. In regard to strategic management, strategic thinking, strategy development, and strategic planning stand out as the crucial divisions of labor that lead to lasting strategy execution. As it pertains to leadership, the clearest model linking practice and performance is one that balances effectiveness with efficiency, aided by the support of good relationships. That kind of model sees the influencing capacity of leadership and the management of activities as mutually necessary for organizational success. Thus armed and loaded, innovation has a chance to hit its mark (if the organizational culture and structures can stimulate and propel innovative development). To simplify the entire leadership practices into a few statements distilling the previous pages, one might say that anticipatory leadership is the practice of leading foresight activities in order to understand the organization's place in the market, what forces it faces, and what it ought to prepare for, that strategic leadership is the practice of leading strategy development and strategic planning efforts in order to select the best paths available at each critical juncture in the near term (such as starting, continuing, or stopping innovative projects), and that administrative leadership is the practice of capturing leftover value through effective management of strategic solutions and creating processes that save organizational resources in order to reinvest them in the anticipatory and strategic leadership practices.

CHAPTER 5

Anticipatory Leadership: Preparing

Most of all, perhaps, we need intimate knowledge of the past. Not that the past has any magic about it, but because we cannot study the future, and yet need something to set against the present, to remind us that the basic assumptions have been quite different in different periods and that much which seems certain to the uneducated is merely temporary fashion.

—C. S. Lewis | "Learning in War Time," in *The Weight of Glory*

The matter of innovation is inherently future-oriented as it directs itself to the "new" and "different," regardless of whether that means new materials, products, or services in whole, part, or use. Often, the latter—that of use—is overlooked, but it bears an increasingly important role among innovating—especially in the pharmaceutical industry, where the creation and patenting of new molecules is increasingly expensive and yielding weaker returns (Philipson and Hult 2015).[1] The reason for its importance is how it relates to framing one's most basic and critical assumptions. Like the illusionary magic of Vaudeville and Vegas, what you see is not necessarily what you get, and that is due to what you see being more a function of "how" you see than a matter of the content itself. To be clear, the subjects of our perceptions are not always fixed, but when they are, how we perceive is critical to our capacity to transmit back that information. For instance, being color-blind makes a difference in our analysis.

---

[1] Philipson, T.J., and K. Hult. April 3, 2015. "Should Investors Pay Attention to the Alleged Productivity Crises in Pharma?" In *American Enterprise Institute*, http://aei.org/publication/should-investors-pay-attention-to-the-alleged-productivity-crises-in-pharma/ (accessed on March 27, 2019).

Our understanding of cultural cues and social norms makes a difference. Our foundational understandings of how the world works and how people relate makes a difference. These are the critical assumptions that affect our interpretation of why business deals succeed or fail, marriages prosper or fall apart, children mature or follow the wrong path, and so on. Thus, it goes without saying that no one arrives at the innovating table without presuppositions about a slew of important concerns. Additionally, and more broadly speaking, no leader or firm approaches the innovation problem without the need to take their presuppositional reality into consideration. For that reason, if you hope to innovate well, you need to learn the practices of anticipatory leadership.

What It Is: The Mindset and Language

Anticipatory leadership, simplified, is the integration of strategic foresight skillsets into the leadership process for the sake of an organization's (good) future. If you remember from the discussion in Chapter 3 about strategic management, strategic foresight is an integral component of the strategic thinking activity. What I am arguing here, then, is that anticipatory leadership is almost exclusively a practice of leadership primed to lead strategic thinking efforts well. That is not to say this leadership practice will not also support and strengthen other strategic management practices. It will. In fact, it is definitely not possible to remove this capacity for action once you have trained in it. Yes, you can forget to apply its principles, but just like how a rubber band, once stretched out, no longer shrinks to the same size, so also will it be difficult for your mind to constrict to its original perspective having already grasped the significant implications of acknowledging and using alternative futures. Furthermore, since I have explained how strategic thinking is an ongoing activity in innovation-minded and strategic-choice-oriented organizations, then anticipatory leadership is both a standalone and an additive leadership paradigm. You can be engaged in anticipatory leadership amid strategic thinking activities, but you can also bring anticipatory leadership into other leadership practices to challenge their inflexibility. Notice what I am not saying: I am not calling anyone to become an anticipatory leader, and neither will I stress strategic leader or administrative leader. My point is that we need integrative leaders. Just as our field stresses the multiplicity of variables that force us into complexity, so also should we recognize the complexity of being a leader. The complexity of our circumstances demands a multiplicity of leadership practices. That is what the integrative leadership model stresses: the multiplicity of demands upon leadership, which anticipatory, strategic, and administrative perspectives provide for.

That being said, you do not need to be positioned as *the* leader to practice strategic foresight and alternative futures framing, but since its successful practice is the objective of strategic thinking, then it logically follows that strategic foresight should be practiced in the leadership context. I believe the field of leadership aims to successfully practice strategic foresight—regardless of whether leaders are studying its application or not—because leadership is a process of influencing to reach a common goal. Such a purpose is innately future-oriented. We can no longer deny that circumstances *will* change from the time we determine the common goal up until the point at which it is reached or that success is no longer an option. We need to accept, therefore, that the minds that can appraise the in-between time best are those which are sharpest in accounting for how many ways everything can go better or worse.

In the realm of leadership, all kinds of mental models take effect. Of the many which target understanding as their goal, focus is generally bounded to either micro, meso, and/or macro contexts. With regard to anticipatory leadership, the driving model is one of external environment evaluation, and the most expansive at that. First, anticipatory leadership is particularly important in helping frame the innovation environment. According to foresight educators Drs. Peter Bishop and Andy Hines, the process of thinking about the future can be divided into four categories with two response categories appended afterward. They are framing, scanning, forecasting, visioning, planning, and acting.[2] The first four deal with understanding:

1. What is the purpose for applying foresight?
2. What is currently driving the future, and what could break that trajectory?

---

[2] Hines, A., and P. Bishop, eds. 2006. *Thinking About The Future: Guidelines For Strategic Foresight*. Washington: Social Technologies, LLC.

3. What futures are most probable, and what are critical measures for monitoring each?
4. What is the most desirable path into the future?

Though each process component is vital to quality outcomes, the scanning component, as mentioned in Chapter 3, is especially important as a feeder activity for the others. The importance of assumptions as the building blocks of organizational and environmental paradigms has been addressed, and so framing, to that end has been introduced.

With framing in place, the scanning activity illustrates how foundational the external environments' cues are for innovation, as they provide the critical resources for innovation decision making. To explain, consider the fairly well-known scanning framework STEEP (social, technological, economical, environmental, political). An acronym for macrocontextual events, ideas, social developments, technological cultivation, political shifts, and more, the STEEP framework, when used in organizational strategy workshops, can help organizations map—and make sense of—large external environments (often, but not necessarily global). The end-game of the STEEP exercise is to generate understanding as to macro-environmental drivers, those currents of change that can shape the landscape of a society and therefore its industries. Such changes can dramatically affect an organization's future if the innovations surrounding an industry are changing at a speed faster or moving in an entirely different direction than the industry itself. The same can be said for how these kinds of drivers can portend conflicts in social values between minority groups and society at large. Such scanning provides the material for intelligent analysis and forecasting (and identifying points of intervention for effective systemic disruption). Against those forecasts, a more enlightened vision for the organization or industry can be considered and mapped out—at least compared to existing organizational or industrywide visions, which may have no qualified basis in the macro-environment.

Second, and building on the importance of gathering and interpreting varied data points, the comprehension of the external environment stems from the goal for strategic foresight—insight for present action. Foresight is external awareness. Condensed, its power is akin to that extra split-second buffer, which providentially leads to a critical swerving away from the future's jack-knifing semi, saving us rather than forcing a family tragedy. Since foresight creates that gap of time, strategic foresight is the wise use of that gap to brace for whatever future arrives. Using the adaptive cycle concept, strategic foresight is the process by which we come to entrepreneurial solutions. In the competitive environment of health care, it helps us ask where we should be applying assets and effort. Like a real-estate mogul speculates what land will be valuable next, so we need to be conscientious speculators as to what values and technologies will be valuable in the future.

One major difference for the health care leader, however, is that this practice of anticipation is a powerful defensive posture to protect our patients against the kind of scarcity that raises costs. Who minds being able to market that their organization saves the city and its patients' time and money, beats industry standards in minimizing the tax burden they place on city residents (if applicable), has higher satisfaction scores, etc.? You should love to brag about the exceptionalism of your organization, but you must think forward and prepare in order to earn those victories. They rarely come by chance. Maybe none of your competitors engage in this either, but neither can they brag about it. No one wins. So take the time to entrench this in practice. Intentionally think about what your future conditions could be like, how different they could look (not just good and bad turns for present issues). Use this to reflect on the efficacy of your operations and how you make strategies. Use it to learn what your role as a future health care organization should be. Use it to identify and make what might be life-saving course corrections before you do not have the capability.

Time Outlook and Perspective

We previously discussed Voros' model and why we need to acquire data for strategic foresight's analysis, interpretation, and prospection, by which we take note of what the future could be like to integrate emerging insights from that vision with the strategy development, planning, and operations of our organizations. One key component to the anticipatory mindset is referred to as time outlook and time perspective. Over twenty years ago, Peg Thoms and David Greenberger published a fascinating journal article in which they considered the relationship between leadership and time orientation.[3] In their research, they discovered that two leadership theories encapsulated a time outlook across the past, present, and future. These were the charismatic leadership theory and a specific formulation of the transformational leadership theory. Other theories that did not relate with all three outlooks but which oriented with at least the future outlook included path-goal theory and entrepreneur role theory. What I hope you can see from that information is that leadership theories implicitly oriented with a future outlook tend to be identifications of leadership that focus on change.

Because our work experiences do not always call for a future orientation, the authors argue that, "individual biases related to the past, present, and future are associated with specific skills needed to perform various tasks typically completed by leaders in situations in which leaders often find themselves," meaning we become inclined to work in the time orientation we operate in most often.[4] For example, if our primary work is leading accounting efforts in our health care organization, then we will likely have a present orientation; while financial asset management may incline us to be more future oriented. It becomes probable, then, that jumping into activities that call for the opposite time outlook will be obstructed by our bias and more difficult for us to learn. In this vein, the authors write that,

> Some tasks, like visioning, planning, goal setting, and motivating are future-oriented tasks and will be performed best by leaders who can warp time, create future schema, and predict. Other tasks, like performance evaluation and problem solving require leaders who can recapture the past.[5]

[3] Thoms, P., and D.B. Greenberger. 1995. "The Relationship between Leadership and Time Orientation." *Journal of Management Inquiry* 4, no. 3, 272–292. *Business Source Complete,* EBSCO*host* (accessed on March 14, 2019).

[4] Ibid., 277.

[5] Thoms, P., and D.B. Greenberger. 1995. "The Relationship between Leadership and Time Orientation." *Journal of Management Inquiry* 4, no. 3, 272–292. *Business Source Complete,* EBSCO*host* (accessed on March 14, 2019).

The purpose of understanding that we, as leaders, have natural comfortability with different time orientations is in recognizing why we might distrust future-oriented tasks—which I hope you understand are vitally important and not to be sluffed off as some kind of imagination games. Moreover, when you take the orientation best aligned for the kind of leadership task at hand, then their research argued you are likely to be more effective in the task completion, that is, you will craft better visions if you can attune to the future, and you will evaluate performance more accurately if you attune to the past. One interesting point that emerged from a related study was that women scored significantly higher than men in regard to holding a future orientation, which should certainly give added credence to your need for a diverse strategic management team.[6]

What the Future Is

The future does not exist. That is both an uninteresting and immensely profound statement. In one sense, we know the future has not yet come to pass, and so it does not *yet* exist; but, in another sense, the future is simply a conception that *only* exists in the present. We can only speak about what is yet to come as "the future" when it is yet to come, and so it never comes into existence. It ever remains out there, somewhere. Please pardon my philosophical drift. I shared that purposefully to help you grasp the complexity of talking about the future and being on the same page with your strategic management team. In order to engage the strategic foresight process and everything that comes with strategic thinking particularly well, you need to be able to have common terminology and expectations for the process. This is difficult with regard to thinking and discussing and deciding about the future.

In essence, there are two schools of thought, and they are based on understanding that previous statement. Within those schools, there is further divergence and nuance, but those two schools remain hinged to assuming either that the future exists as an object headed toward the

---

[6] Zimbardo, P.G., and J.N. Boyd. 1999. "Putting Time in Perspective: A Valid, Reliable Individual-Differences Metric." *Journal of Personality and Social Psychology* 77, no. 6, pp. 1271–1288.

present, being knowable or unknowable but nonetheless real, or that the future is a mental illusion, just a useful conceit for untethering us from widely held assumptions. The former deals with questions of knowing, and the latter deals with questions of being. As it pertains to health care organizations, both schools of thought are necessary. Such a strong opinion might frighten my colleagues, because we have to choose, right? Wrong. We have to understand and use each appropriately in this instance. These are assumptions that define how we perceive, like lenses that determine color shading, and unlike lenses that determine clarity. Let me give you a couple of reasons why you need them both. First, the school that recognizes the future as a fact headed for *now* is a school that can motivate present action to shape it or reshape their own organization in expectation of its arrival. The school that denies the future as having *being* outside of the present grants us freedom from the notion that a particularly imagined future is unavoidable or predetermined for us. In these ways, both schools promote a freedom to act in the present with creative legitimacy.[7]

Second, one school gives us a power to plan through its assumptions about probability and forecasting while the second gives us the power intelligently break with plans and acknowledge the power of creative activity to generate the present, that is, one school promotes trajectory alignment and future-capture whereas the other promotes present-expansion. Futures expert Riel Miller explains the argument for what I call the second school this way:

> The challenge is not to find better ways to "know" the future; rather we need to find ways to embrace the creative novelty that is at the origin of not-knowing the future...The point is not to find methods for attacking, overcoming or reducing the unknown. Rather the goal is to accept and use the unknown, to sustain it and still exercise our intention and volition (Ogilvy, 2010). The

---

[7] Miller, R. 2011. "Being without Existing: The Futures Community at a Turning Point? A Comment." *Foresight* 13, no. 4, 24–34. *EconLit with Full Text,* EBSCO*host* (accessed on July 8, 2018).

bottom line is that ... to create a better world we need to change how we think about the future not what.[8]

In that sense, the future is a tool for learning about how we think, how we plan, what we fear, and what we value. It helps us uncover what lay hidden beneath the surface of our decision making as well as gives us more robust understanding regarding our organization's mission and vision. As health care leaders, such exercises are vital to ensure we do not lose our aim to serve with the utmost integrity. It would be tragic to find ourselves falsely enslaved, operating to serve a nonexistent master at the cost of our souls.

What It Does: The Tools

Social Change Theory

The tools that might be used in the practice of anticipatory leadership are legion. They could range from big data analytics and census surveys to imaginative exercises like storytelling. Below, therefore, I will highlight a few of what I consider the most useful introductory tools for thinking strategically in order to lead with an anticipative posture. To begin, it would be helpful for you to have a basic working knowledge and usable framework of key theories of social change, since innovating is ultimately focused on the adoption of innovations in key segments of, or across all of, society. There are at least four broad categories of such theories: evolutionary, conflict, structural-functional, and social-psychological.[9] Have no fear, there will be no tests! In simplified terms, the first deals with the notion that society moves from lesser to greater complexity and differentiation. The second posits the notion that competition for scarce resources elicits change; the third argues for a systems approach where changes occur as the offsetting of other societal changes in an effort to maintain balance; and the fourth points to individuals' behavioral shifts as the

---

[8] Ibid, 29.

[9] Vago, S. 2004. *Social Change,* 49–79, 5th ed. Upper Saddle River, NJ: Pearson Prentice Hall.

impetus for cascading change (little changes in behavior adding up). The value in understanding these four kinds of social change is that by understanding them, you can use them. You can make plausible assumptions about the future according to how society changes. This is why social change matters to you, because you can expect change to follow a pattern or roadmap. The future will be expected to bend in a certain direction, by a certain amount, so often, with a certain kind of ignition. As you grasp why change occurs, then you will likely have a better shot in crafting innovations that are more readily adoptable.

In addition, if forecasts of society at large can be argued for or against, then so can strategies for innovation in response, that is, you can set a strategy intentionally crafted for effective adoption based on the kind of social change assumptions you are operating under. By that I mean if you can argue for a particular change pattern across larger social segments, then you may also argue for the need to innovate in order to meet that change head-on or to utilize that change for your competitive advantage. But, caveat emptor, if the theory of change that undergirds your forecasting is inaccurate, meaning reality did not care about your expectations and decided to run rampant upon your assumptions, then your forecasts will be off and your innovation assumptions potentially worthless. Of course, in your organization, your innovations may be of a smaller variety, pertaining mostly to how you organize staff and schedule, what kinds of team practices you engage in to save time and increase communication across units, craft marketing efforts that draw in clients with substantially higher conversion rates, the kind that affect your local or regional market but are not likely to reshape your industry. This does not mean the innovation emphasis within your organization should diminish; rather, it means your organization may actually be somewhat more protected from the kinds of innovation that would—to their fault—rely on those faulty forecast assumptions. The reason I say this is that your innovation efforts will likely be those you can afford and the kind you believe will be necessary according to your forecasting. Based on your forecasts, you will do what your resources permit, and so in all likelihood, the innovations you deploy will be in relation to personnel and assets you can use differently than others. Only a handful of you will be innovating with regard to high-value technical assets and that is perfectly normal. We have grown into a society that thinks innovation and technology are automatically *only* industry-rocking and computer-oriented, but if you remember points in Chapter 2, innovation relates to business model changes at least as much as it does to technology changes. Even with regard to technology, innovation is less about the technology itself and more about how it is used. The better use of information rather than the hard *material* is the value-adding component that innovation offers, that is, it is no longer the microprocessor that most often makes the greatest difference; now it is the software running them and running on them that alters the computing landscape most. Here is one last comment on these theories as you watch your own industry and your competitors within it, and especially as you monitor their future-focused decisions: unity regarding what view is the dominant theory of social change in effect will be critical to innovation-making processes and resulting activities. The more robust an organization's future view, the more likely its engagement in innovation making will not follow simple predictions, and the more competitive its offerings can become. Thus, even having a rudimentary understanding of those four theories and why social change is an important field of study for anticipatory leadership will benefit you more than you can yet imagine.

Scenario Planning

Scenarios are fictional glimpses of the future. They are not prophecies or predictions, since the former should never be fictional and the latter go beyond the intent of scenario planning. Rather, scenarios are useful in strategic thinking efforts because looking at strategy concerns through various scenarios provides decision makers with a view as to how strategic maneuvers may play out, especially valuable in modern, unpredictable arenas like health care. Scenarios, therefore, provide imagined environments for gaming present strategies in order to identify weaknesses in our assumptions, highlight our blind spots, and locate untapped potential. There are three reasons to use scenarios: (1) to discuss big issues about the future, (2) to plan for the future, and (3) to enrich organizational learning. When current strategies are gamed through the alternative futures which scenarios represent, team members are forced to logically embrace a greater awareness of how varying macro-environmental factors could interact with their planned decision-paths—how plausible events and developments could enhance, paralyze, hinder, undo, support, and/or make obsolete their organizational work. However, since scenarios are not predictions, scenarios are not games "to win." They are more like pregame warmups—stretching exercises—for the sake of enhancing adaptability and agility for the real thing. Here is a simplified process for scenario development.

Identify the Driving Forces of Change

Our environments are rich with fads and trends, the former dying out quickly with little impact and the latter showing up earlier than anyone routinely observes, lasting beyond their significance, and ultimately having the potential to converge as forces that change our world. These trends can generally be categorized into the five STEEP macro-environmental domains. The higher a trend's impact-probability mix is, the more closely it needs to be monitored, and the more central role it needs to play in our set of scenarios. Note: in Figure 5.1, the "zone of significant concern" below is not located further left, because the probabilities become too low to justify consideration while trend tracking bears out other concerns (i.e., evidence is too difficult to come by, which is why these surprise us), and it is not further right since current strategies already account for known high-probability trends. Finally, low-impact areas are important, but not of strategic concern.

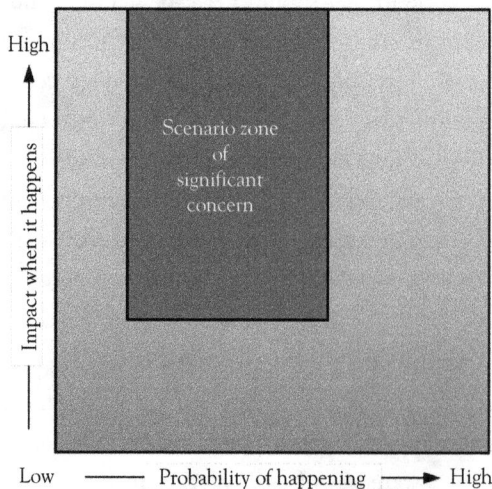

Figure 5.1 Impact probability diagram

Highlight Critical Uncertainties

While scenarios can be prepared in a number of different ways, for our purposes we utilize the axes of uncertainty method as follows:

1. Group clusters of related, documented trends according to perceived patterns. Use these to visualize driving forces.
2. Identify two high-impact clusters with competing trends, which could drive the future one way or the other. Such suggests the forces are highly sensitive and reciprocally responsive.
3. Plot these two high-impact, uncertain force clusters as polar continuums (i.e., low–high, poor–rich, big–small, fast–slow, happy–sad)
4. Create a four-quadrant grid by superimposing one of the continuums perpendicular to the other (Figure 5.2).

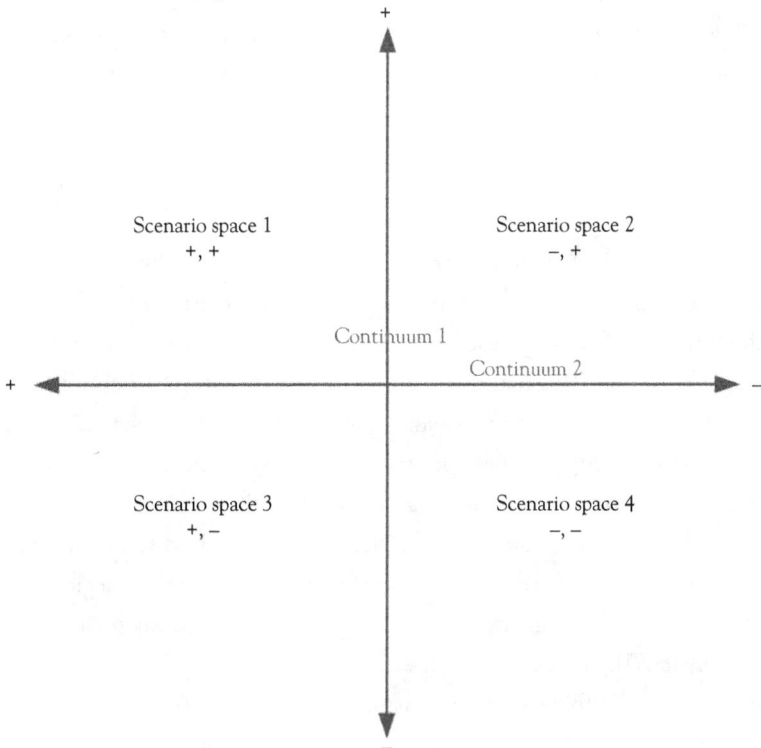

Figure 5.2 Four-quadrant scenario space

Map Plausible Scenarios

These resultant quadrants are scenario spaces, building upon the logic of our combined critical uncertainties. Note that scenario-crafting is a skill. Not all scenarios are useful. Good scenario sets entail: (1) the robust ability to provide insights for decisions under review, (2) realistically possible futures, (3) the maintenance of some probability for each scenario, (4) logically consistent emergence for the scenarios, (5) qualitative difference between scenarios, (6) memorability of scenario diversity, and (7) a strong challenge to organizational assumptions.

Choose Strategic Issues to Stress

Finally, the goal of scenario-crafting is to stress test the organization's current or intended strategy against the scenarios and the dilemma's and windfalls they present. The ultimate aim, as mentioned earlier, is not to win the scenario. Instead, like stretching, stress testing with scenarios is a way to maintain your strategic agility as a health care organization. It helps you to think quickly about contingencies and stretches your creative capacity to interpret widely varying events.

Futures Wheels

The futures wheel (Figure 5.3) is a tool for organizing how you think about the future, and it provides you with a way to ask questions about the future and construct useful answers. Perhaps you have seen web-like diagrams before. This tool will share some of the characteristics of brainstorming tools like mind maps and spider diagrams, but it has a unique foresight use, and that pertains to modeling systemic consequences— systemic, meaning that a single cause has more than a single effect. This tool helps reveal the complex interrelationships that lead to our futures, and prompts future consciousness in the operational and strategic work of health care. You start by, as a team, agreeing unanimously on a potential impact. Then, you choose three STEEP domains for considering the impact. That is followed by brainstorming to agreement on three consequences from the initial impact, one for each domain. That process repeats for the subsequent domains, as each consequence from the initial

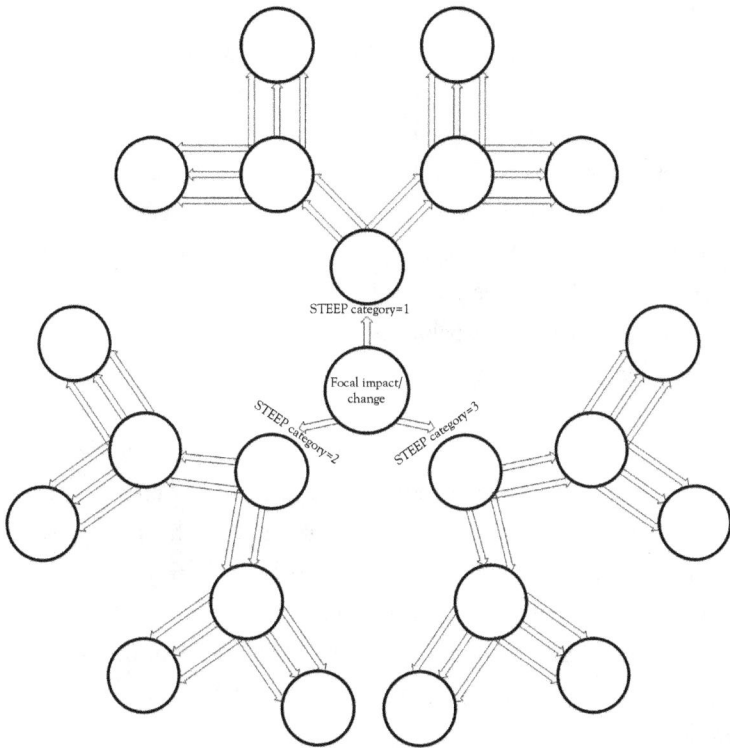

STEEP category=1

Focal impact/ change

STEEP category=2

STEEP category=3

Figure 5.3 Futures wheel

impact now functions as an initial impact for even farther-reaching consequences. From the activity, you can discuss the length of time that would necessarily take place between impacts and consequences, whether patterns emerge from the changes, how difficult it is to creatively imagine consequences in various domains, and how consequences reflect the assumptions undergirding our judgments rather than causal relationships.

Summary

Here is another way of thinking about strategic foresight, the interpretation, and translation force behind strategic thinking and the anticipatory leadership that promotes it: Strategic foresight, being a metaphoric competency, a hermeneutic process, is raw strategy's insurance policy, its hedge. Moreover, Cornish notes, "foresight enables us to anticipate many of the risks and opportunities that could confront us in the future, giving us the time to decide what to do before we crash into them."[10] Of course, this kind of description might lead one to think that foresight *is* strategic management itself, but it is not. It is a component of strategic thinking. However, in broad terms, strategy formulates the organization's direction, while foresight monitors the enterprise's current and possible future operating conditions. Thus, strategic foresight merges well with strategy work, but it is broader and more inquisitive when compared to strategy's more declarative nature. In watercraft terms, strategy attends to the vessel's navigation capabilities (motor, rotor, computers, hull, and so on), whereas foresight observes, records, and postulates upon how the seas interact with (thwarting, forcing, and ignoring), and *could* interact with, the vessel. One might ultimately call foresight the skill of consideration, the entertainment of possibilities for the sake of present situation enhancement. It is the satellite and radar technology that integrates with the ship's mapping systems and the captain's know-how and route intentions for the sake of contingency planning. Thus, the leadership practices leveraging strategic foresight are anticipatory. It is inquiring now as to what may come next, comparing that data against regular cycles of change and development, and generating various interpretations of the results. Such leaders are not trying to predict the future—as that would be reckless since it is impossible—but they are trying to prepare for it. Thus, the interpretations they generate, often in the form of scenarios, are varied in order to provide paradigm-busting visions for their organizations' and industries' strategy teams. In the next section related to strategic leadership, the leadership process—as it pertains specially to innovation—encounters strategic planning. And, planners without a robust comprehension of the futures' zigs and zags will likely run into a ditch, not having developed the necessary strategic agility that the practice of anticipatory leadership cultivates.

---

[10] Cornish, E. 2004. *Futuring: The Exploration of the Future*, xi. Bethesda, MD: World Future Society.

CHAPTER 6

Strategic Leadership: Prioritizing

Strategy means making clear-cut choices about how to compete.
—Jack Welch | former CEO, General Electric

With the tools and mindset of strategic foresight in place through anticipatory leadership, the conditions are met for the onset of strategic leadership to take the reins. What separates this set of leadership practices from others is that it encompasses thought, action, and influence in the leadership process for the explicit purpose of promoting "the sustainable competitive advantage of the organization."[1] Again, this ties together the thread of the future and the present developed with anticipatory leadership, since competitive advantage is the primary aim of organizations and industries seeking to win the war of creating value through scarce resources. Moreover, that the effort needs to be sustainable illustrates the inherent application of resource management with the leadership process, that is, these are the leadership practices that prioritize choices for maximum impact in long-term organizational endeavors.

What It Is: The Mindset and Language

Strategic leadership is the wide and deep view to organizational and industrywide matters. Anticipatory leadership, in contrast, practiced a much broader domain sweep for issues of importance. The leadership process, therefore, is strategic if it functions with a systemic perspective, where issues are not viewed in isolation or considered important solely

---

[1] Hughes, R.L., and K.C. Beatty. 2005. *Becoming a Strategic Leader: Your Role in Your Organization's Enduring Success.* San Francisco: Jossey-Bass.

based on proximity to the present. To some degree, the leader would see time as a single variable with more or less importance to an issue only in connection with other variables, also having more or less value in present decision making themselves. In practice, this means you view the health care industry from a long time horizon and your organization within it the same way. This is not the same kind of practice as what anticipatory leadership promotes, because it remains constrained to your competitive positioning within the industry. To visualize it, consider the health care industry as a baby that grows over time. Consider your organization as being responsible for dressing the child as he grows. Anticipatory leadership could give you signals to what kinds of clothes are in fashion, what fabrics are ethically sourced, how the climate is changing, and more; but, strategic leadership would make the decisions of choosing which clothes the boy wears, when it is time to purchase larger sizes, makes the mistakes of picking out-of-style outfits, and indulges in better fabrics to protect him or provide more comfort.

Since the time horizon of the strategic leadership practice is similar to anticipatory leadership, though, they do mutually support and strengthen each other's process. At the same time, however, you need to be mindful that strategic leadership's thoughts about the industry's future are not forecasts, or are bad ones if accepted. The reasoning here is that strategic leadership's forward perspective is built upon anticipatory leadership providing alternative futures for it to think through. For example, once strategic leadership has the fleshed-out scenarios or futures wheel or trend map created through anticipatory leadership, it can then consider how its organization and industry will be shaped by and react to such changes. But those notions will have been based on explicit or implicit assumptions from the alternative futures creation practice. They are not predictions. They are not facts. Leaders who practice strategic leadership well will understand this, and their decisions will be couched in risk management, knowing their primary concerns, core competencies, and which uncertainties could derail the agenda.

Moreover, because of this long-view toward the organization, such leadership is powerful in enacting systemic, disruptive change. However, as argued, that change is aimed at long-term, sustainable competitive advantage and not faddish market engagement. Change in health care is difficult enough. We do not need a hyped tactic that results in a few units having a bit more enthusiasm for a couple months while senior leadership looks on and pats themselves on the back for doing something talked about in a CEO magazine. Deep change is rarely glamorous or easy. Furthermore, some major impediments to such leadership practices exist, particularly in the form of waning focus, unaligned tactics, and near-sightedness. The first is catastrophic as it ruptures the key element of strategic leadership, which is prioritization for sustainable competitive advantage. You need full commitment. The second, likewise, detrimentally keeps the organization from affecting an advantage by limiting the result of otherwise concerted efforts. You need the synergy that comes from mutually edifying efforts across the organization. The third, finally, cuts the legs out from under competitiveness by sacrificing tomorrow's ace for today's par, sacrificing rooks to capture pawns. You need to think of your organization like we hope patients think of their own well-being, with the lifelong victory superseding the tantalizing siren's song of short-term indulgence.

Undergirding this practice of leadership and propelling leaders of the sort forward are ways of thinking, acting, and influencing. These efforts aim to promote change in organizations through reinforcing loops, that is, the strategic leader sustains competitive advantage by leveraging each past change to the benefit of each present change effort toward the goal of a stronger, more successful organizational future. For instance, suppose your strategy has a specific component relating to the time it takes to move a patient through the check-in process, then strategic thinking on this point would identify options that could promote increasing the speed through personnel training, more effective technology, clearer direction, or reducing extraneous actions. Strategic action would emerge through testing the best supported options, and strategic influencing would be demonstrated in helping the front-desk personnel to desire the added-value as much as leadership and see themselves as owners of that link in the value chain. The same kind of framework could be applied in a pharmaceutical development process. Moreover, the chief driver of this loop (options, actions, and influence) is a learning cycle emphasizing assessment, understanding, learning, activity, and evaluation. In effect, it is the scientific method applied to organizational endeavors with the emphasis on results—and that is what the integrative leadership model is focused on, outstanding health care outcomes.

One way to understand the strategic leadership process is linearly, by steps. I have pushed the notion that these practices of leadership, like the adaptive cycles, are always-on, akin to an electronic device being in a low-energy state and always ready to perform. At the same time, I have argued that these practices might not be practiced in an orderly fashion, because if your organizations are anything like mine have been, then you have many organizational units operating simultaneously without fear of the chaos committed by overlapping. They do cause problems, but that is a complexity we have to deal with, not a complication that can be solved. Still, we often understand linear progression best (at least in the West). With that all being said, similar to Phase 1 acquisition in the strategic thinking step of strategic management (Chapter 3), the first step of practicing strategic leadership is aggregating pertinent information for the organization's strategy making, since strategic leadership and strategy making go hand in hand. The difference between the two, remember, is scope (domain for foresight needs versus organization/industry for strategy needs). In the second step, the organization's values come into play so that alignment in sustainable competitive advantage is not handicapped by unclear vision, mission, and core values statements.[2] The third step is taking place when organizational needs are differentiated, ensuring the discovery of the overall strategy's most important components to sustainable competitive advantage. The fourth and final step of practicing strategic leadership occurs when the leader takes the organization through the implementation stage, which is the ultimate testing ground for their work. Afterward, the organization needs to process the strategy's effectiveness, for which after-action reports can offer new insight pertaining to the implementation. Reflections like these play a significant role in the practices of administrative leadership.

By distilling that process, we find that the work of those committed to strategic leadership is, in essence, to take up the challenge to create focus,

---

[2] Hughes, R.L., and K.C. Beatty. 2005. *Becoming a Strategic Leader: Your Role in Your Organization's Enduring Success.* San Francisco: Jossey-Bass.

the challenge to align tactics with strategy, and the challenge to keep the long term in mind despite short-term pressures. Strategic thinking continues to play a significant role in the cognitive dimension of such leadership, including discerning which environmental trends have strategic significance for your organization, sifting through waves of information to identify the most strategically significant facts or issues upon which decisions need to be made, as well as viewing emerging opportunities and threats from multiple perspectives, and recognizing the ways units and departments contribute to an integrated whole. The behavior component is strategic acting, and as addressed in the introduction to leadership, proves it is not so much what one says, but what one does that reverberates loudest. For strategy to matter, therefore, and not just be a spiral bound booklet that gathers dust, leadership behaviors must make it so. Strategic action is about behaving in a manner that is consistent with the strategic direction of the organization, that is, how leaders lead despite the ambiguity, complexity, and chaos inherent in lives of healthcare organizations. Such actions are strategic if "it is reasonable to expect they will impact the organization's sustainable competitive advantage."[3] As an example, relative to your sales processes, spending time to evaluate and money to secure a new network of channels through which to sell is strategic if diversification of vendors and customer segments is inherent to organizational strategy for long-term success. In choosing when and where to act, these leaders ask questions like: "Which new project will offer the greater long-term advantage?," "Whom do you appoint to lead the new corporate innovation team?," and "What stand should your company take with regard to questions being raised about its environmental impact?"[4]

Leaders who find success in strategy making and implementation are those who are open to others and to whom others are open, engaging in discussion, and the transfer of ideas throughout the organizational structures. If information flows down from you alone, then your hierarchy may be effective, but it will not encourage cooperation, a hallmark of

---

[3] Hughes, R.L., and K.C. Beatty. 2005. *Becoming a Strategic Leader: Your Role in Your Organization's Enduring Success*, 85–86. San Francisco: Jossey-Bass.

[4] Ibid, 85.

successful change management. Without the capacity to change—because of the bottleneck permitting information to only flow in one direction— your organization will not have the agility to sense at the periphery, which rarely concerns just top operators. Of course, top leaders do have positional authority that should send their information through the system faster, bypassing gatekeepers in ways that information flowing up to supervisors and across to peers will not necessarily be as uninhibited. Such is the cost of vetting information, since collaboration does impede efficiency temporarily. At the same time, so also does bad information and decrees from leadership established by harmful assumptions.

You either pay to have more alertness through better information flow sooner, or you pay because you were unaware later on. Strategic influence offers an answer, therefore, and gives traction to organizational change processes. In addition, because multiple interests are usually at stake, it is important to leverage the strength of teams in the efforts for strategic change. Collaborating with others, who also do not know everything, but who may know something you do not, and who can contribute to leading strategic change, is vital to strategy implementation and success. Similarly, strategic leadership recognizes that culture matters. Moreover, some environments are more conducive to developing this kind of strategic leadership and strategic change capability. You may not be able to forcefully generate this kind of culture, but if you recognize its emergence, then you will be able to appreciate its value more than the unaware. Furthermore, you would have an immediate understanding of how you need to behave so that you can encourage the collaborative atmosphere to ripen and proliferate to your advantage.

In real time, the activity seems much more disordered. In competitive environments, organizations are acting and reacting to each other's competitive actions, adjusting their activities accordingly. You can only engage your environment excellently, then, if you have already deployed solid anticipatory leadership practices. They will give proper attention to the changes occurring in the macro and microenvironments so that you can respond appropriately. That is how your organization will move forward and remain aligned with what satisfies your customers/clients/ patrons while providing it in a way that sustains your organization financially. Thus, for the strategic leader, great confidence and competency in performing strategy development work is crucial. Henry Mintzberg, a noted strategy expert and scholar with whose work many of the preceding chapters' ideas about strategy resonate, identified with Bruce Ahlstrand and Joseph Lampel, five general understandings of what is meant by "strategy.[5]" These include strategy as:

- A plan: Directions for intended *future* behavior.
- A pattern: Evidence of behavior consistent with *past* actions.
- A position: Location of one's organization or its products and services in relation to the rest of his industry's market, this looks *outward* to examine the market.
- A perspective: The organization's theory of how business is done, which looks *inward* to see how the organization operates.
- A ploy: Maneuvers as actions in the action-reaction game with competitors.

To break this down from the vantage point of strategic leadership practices, positioning and ploy take precedence for answering what the purpose of strategy making is, and planning helps guide the organization in particular directions given the specifics of its internal and external environments. Alternatively, pattern and perspective give insight for interpreting strategies and evaluating their intentions and results. The strategic leader, then, is to conduct strategy development and implementation with the perspective something like that of a physician giving a medical exam. First, the doctor runs tests and analyzes the patients' current conditions in order to best understand what is affecting them. He is also checking their responses to particular stimuli. Second, he offers his diagnosis of their health, explaining why they might feel a certain way or why they are responding to the environment as they are. Third, based on his diagnosis, given because of the examination results, he delivers his prescription—what needs to be done in order to properly address the current conditions.

---

[5] Mintzberg, H., B. Ahlstrand, and J. Lampel. 2005. *Strategy Safari; A Guided Tour Through the Wilds of Strategic Management*, 9–15. New York, NY: The Free Press.

Because of their iterative, cyclically building nature, strategic leadership practices can only excel to the level that the organizational strategy allows. In addition, in the words of Kluyver and Pearce II, the strategy formulation process is just as iterative and learning-focused as strategic leadership itself:

> Strategy formulation is about crafting a long-term vision for an organization while maintaining a degree of flexibility about how to get there and creating a portfolio of options for adapting to change. Learning is an essential component of this process. As soon as a company begins to implement a chosen direction, it starts to learn—about how well attuned the direction is to the competitive environment, how rivals are likely to respond, and how well prepared the organization is to carry out its competitive intentions.[6]

Given the competitive environment, there are considered to be two generic strategies organizational leaders can embark upon, and three more with a bit of added complexity:

1. *Low-cost provider strategy*: Aims to lower overall costs compared to one's market rivals in an appeal to gaining larger market share—usually through cost efficiency or revolutionary overhaul of the value chain.
2. *Broad differentiation strategy*: Aims to make the organization's value proposition different from market rivals—usually through combining value for the user, raising performance, increasing intangible benefits, and/or adding distinctive capabilities to products/services, which competitors cannot provide cost-effectively.
3. *Best-cost provider strategy*: Aims to increase user value with near-equal quality and lower cost than the market's quality leaders—usually through a cheaper cost of feature inclusion, economies of scale in production or development, and/or customer service supremacy.

---

[6] De Kluyver, C.A., and J.A. Pearce II. 2012. *Strategy: A View From The Top*, 8. 4th ed. Upper Saddle River, NJ: Prentice Hall.

4. *Focused (or market niche) strategy based on low costs*: Aims to win a specific group of users with lower prices through lower provision costs for that segment.

5. *Focused (or market niche) strategy based on differentiation*: Aims to attract a specific group with specialized attributes more desirable than rivals' offerings.[7]

To bring this together, leaders exercising strategic leadership will be capable of employing both the organization's business strategy and leadership strategy equally well, where the former ensures the organization's approach to strategic drivers is focused and can leverage market advantages and the latter bolsters the business strategy with the right people and mental models.[8] Let us now consider some tools that bolster the mindset and desired outcomes of strategic leadership.

What It Does: The Tools

OCAI and MSAI: *Organizational Culture and Management Skills Assessment Instruments*

Critical to the success of strategic endeavors, the fostering of a strategically managed organization, and the persistent systems-thinking approach to action, is the nurturing of the proper organizational culture within your organization. One dominant culture already exists where you lead, but is it rich in the kinds of values and assumptions that drive the health care innovation efforts you need now or will need in the near future? Management and organization experts Kim Cameron and Robert Quinn explain:

> Understanding organizational culture is important because it is the single largest factor that inhibits organizational improvement and change. Research is clear that healthy cultures enhance success whereas unhealthy cultures inhibit success, but in order to

---

[7] Thompson Jr., A.A., A.J. Strickland III, and J.E. Gamble. 2010. *Crafting and Executing Strategy*, 140–141, 17th ed. New York: McGraw-Hill/Irwin.

[8] Hughes, R.L., and K.C. Beatty. 2005. *Becoming a Strategic Leader: Your Role in Your Organization's Enduring Success*. San Francisco: Jossey-Bass.

take advantage of the power of organizational culture, it must be adequately measured.[9]

Social science has generated countless studies as to what differences exist between organizations that die, those that merely survive, and those that thrive. And, the key difference, they point out, is having an organizational culture (read: environment, a way of doing things, an ethos, a character, etc.) aligned to the necessary competencies of their line of work, that is, if they are high-tech developers, then they have a culture encouraging decentralized decision making and innovative problem-solving without oppressive hierarchical, regulatory pushback; but, if they are a governmental agency, then the culture encourages mechanisms of control which force deliberation and encourage decision-contemplation and discourage reckless actions.[10] The purposed strength of culture, then, is in:

- *"Reducing collective uncertainties"*—facilitating a common interpretation system;
- *"Creating social order"*—clarifying member expectations;
- *"Creating continuity"*—perpetuating organizational values in subsequent generations;
- *"Creating a collective identity and commitment"*—congealing membership; and
- *"Clarifying the organization's future vision"*—motivating for progress.[11]

Scarce resources will always present an organizational challenge, but we rarely think of them positively, usually focusing on what is given up rather than on what is gained. But, trade-offs can be viewed as not only

---

[9] Cameron, K.S., and R.E. Quinn. 2011b. *The Competing Values Culture Assessment: Culture Assessment Workbook.* In *Jossey-Bass,* 5–6. Available from http://josseybass.com/go/cameron (accessed on June 25, 2013).

[10] Deal, T.E., and A.A. Kennedy. 1982. *Corporate Cultures: The Rights and Rituals of Corporate Life.* Reading, MA: Addison-Wesley.

[11] Cameron, K.S., and R.E. Quinn. 2011a. *Diagnosing and Changing Organizational Culture: Based on the Competing Values Framework,* 6, 3rd ed. San Francisco: John Wiley and Sons.

necessary, but also be perceived as good for maximizing the impact of what we have and what we can do with such. In the same way, cultures present value trade-offs in action. We may value stability and control, but that will come at the expense of flexibility and discretion in decision making. Both are desirable organizational values; but, depending on the kind of work we are engaged in and the expectations under which we operate, those values are going to remain at odds, and one will likely dominate.

Cameron and Quinn, the preeminent scholar-practitioners who developed the Organization Culture Assessment Instrument and the Management Skills Assessment Instrument, have conducted much of the pivotal research on how to diagnose and change organizational cultures in reference to what is called the competing values framework (CVF). This framework is constructed as a 2 × 2 matrix with four quadrants, each representing a culture type. They note from their research:

> Some organizations were effective if they demonstrated flexibility and adaptability, but other organizations were effective if they demonstrated stability and control. Similarly, some organizations were effective if they maintained efficient internal processes whereas others were effective if they maintained competitive external positioning relative to customers and clients.[12]

Essentially, when you combine an internal focus that is integrative with a capacity for flexibility and discretion, the organization tends to operate collaboratively, like a clan. When such flexibility and discretion is mixed with an external focus and differentiating perspective, the organization tends to be creative and functions like an adhocracy. Alternatively, when the organization is more stability-minded and control-oriented, the organizations could be either hierarchical (internal focus and integrating) or market-like (external focus and differentiating).[13]

---

[12] Cameron, K.S., and R.E. Quinn. 2011b. *The Competing Values Culture Assessment: Culture Assessment Workbook.* In *Jossey-Bass,* 3. Available from http://josseybass.com/go/cameron (accessed on June 25, 2013).

[13] Cameron, K.S., and R.E. Quinn. 2011a. *Diagnosing and Changing Organizational Culture: Based on the Competing Values Framework,* 39, 3rd ed. San Francisco: John Wiley and Sons.

In brief, the quadrants represent our personal perceptions at the axes. In regard to how this looks in practice, starting with Clan, we will do things together in pursuit of long-term development, even if waiting to get everyone aboard delays progress. In adhocracy, we aim to do things first to secure breakthroughs. As an observation, from the start you should notice how these two quadrants align with the "cooperate" and "autonomy" means of interaction as expressed in Robert Keidel's triadic model approach to organization design (from Chapter 4). In the Market quadrant, we aim to do things fast to perform well in the short term. Finally, in the Control quadrant we aim to do things right, increasing performance incrementally. With culture-making and shifting, the various time-bound objectives that can help your organization reach its innovation and sustainability goals become vastly more reachable. Without the alertness to how your culture may be hindering your efforts to enhance cooperation, innovation, competitive offerings, or establish particular operations policies, you will have a hard time motivating change, and you will not be evidencing strategic leadership.

Each of these cultural types is driven by a theory about what organizational effectiveness consists in, and it is that theory and its supporting values that leaders and behaviors promote.[14] For example, clan cultures promote the idea that collaboration and human development yield effectiveness. For adhocracy cultures, the drivers are innovation mindedness, strategic vision, and new resources. For market cultures, the drivers are an underlying competitiveness and service orientation. For hierarchy cultures, control and efficiency wedded to competency in operational processes are the keys to effectiveness. Of important note is that Cameron and Quinn identified what seemed to them to be organizational trends across the organizational lifecycle. For example, they suggest that top managers usually identify with the profile of a clan culture. Another finding was that adhocracy tends to be rarest among cultural identification. Hierarchy and market culture types were dominant over time, illustrating in their model a kind of "gravity" where organizations fall from the top quadrants

---

[14] Cameron, K.S., and R.E. Quinn. 2011a. *Diagnosing and Changing Organizational Culture: Based on the Competing Values Framework.* 3rd ed. San Francisco: John Wiley and Sons.

and find it increasingly difficult to regain the flexibility and discretion that situated them in the upper quadrants. One more apparent trend that is highly significant for our purposes pertains to how effective organizations have leadership that emphasizes the dichotomies appropriately rather than arguing for a singular position of change or stability.[15]

Unmentioned at this point has been the MSAI, which focuses on the critical managerial competencies that align with each culture type.[16] Once again, the research bears evidence highlighting the value of adaption, flexibility, and integration, in that particular competencies are best leveraged when aligned with particular culture types. For clan cultures, these are managing teams, interpersonal relationships, and the development of others. For adhocracy cultures, these are managing innovation, the future, and continuous improvement. For market cultures, these are managing competitiveness, customer service, and energizing employees. Lastly, for hierarchy cultures, the critical managerial competencies are managing acculturation, the control system, and coordination. Cameron and Quinn tell us that the MSAI, in measuring behaviors is not presenting a premise like many other assessments related to leadership that promotes a certain style or attitude as the crux of organizational effectiveness. Instead, their assessment operates under the assumption that critical, culturally aligned behaviors promote organizational effectiveness, and so regardless of a leader/manager's established personality, style, or attitude, their behaviors are the chief determinant of their effectiveness outcomes. In the same way, the integrative leadership model promotes the idea of practices being central to outstanding health care outcomes because changes and adjustments are observable, interpretable, debatable, and measurable. Thus, in same way that culture changes when behavior changes, so also organizational outcomes change as leadership practices change.

---

[15] Cameron, K.S., and R.E. Quinn. 2011a. *Diagnosing and Changing Organizational Culture: Based on the Competing Values Framework,* 3rd ed. San Francisco: John Wiley and Sons.
[16] Ibid.

The Baldrige Excellence Framework

I assume that many of you are familiar with, have heard of, or even are deeply involved in the implementation of recommendations flowing from the Baldrige Excellence Framework's Health Care Criteria for Performance Excellence. If not, then you need to secure a copy of the most recent document (the 2021–2022 edition will be available in mid-January 2021.) and establish a team to consider its use. It is more than qualified as a framework for helping organizations achieve their strategic pursuits, and their focused approach to healthcare only makes their framework more worthwhile. Remember how strategic leadership, unlike anticipatory leadership, narrowed the domain focus for the internal and external environmental changes? Well, there may not be a better constraining device than this framework and criteria for evaluating your organization across multiple dimensions. In the program's own words, its purpose is to help you answer these questions:

1. "Is your organization doing as well as it could?
2. How do you know?
3. What and how should your organization improve or change?"[17]

The four dimensions along which the framework can help you consider these questions in light of your current organizational processes start with the approach you take to crafting or choosing effective methods and practices. Thus, the Baldrige Framework, encouraging a systems perspective to organizational ecosystems, aligns well with the integrative leadership model. The second dimension is that of deployment, giving you the go-ahead to ask whether you have execution processes, how they are faring, what can be done better, and what should be discarded. Third, you are encouraged to assess your learning processes, calling into question whether your organization is intent on capturing knowledge it gains

---

[17] Baldrige Performance Excellence Program. 2015. *2015–2016 Baldrige Excellence Framework: A Systems Approach to Improving Your Organization's Performance (Health Care)*, ii. Gaithersburg, MD: U.S. Department of Commerce, National Institute of Standards and Technology. http://nist.gov/baldrige

and putting those gains to work. The fourth dimension is integration, gauging how aligned your processes are so that synergies—rather than constraints—are accrued.

Also, like the MSAI, the Baldrige Framework is ultimately focused on results—what different perspectives about our organization say about our organization's behavior. For healthcare, the framework asks:

- How do your patients, other customers, and other stakeholders view you?
- How efficient and effective are your operations?
- Is your organization learning and growing?[18]

Organizing their framework linearly would not be appropriate, given it is an assessment support tool as well as a kind of strategy in its own right. It consists of a leadership triad that evidences how leadership practices focus on customers and the strategy by which the organization relates to them. Second is the results triad, which pertains to how the combination of the workforce and operations processes produce results of all kinds (personnel, financial, leadership, competitive). The context for these triads is the organizational profile describing the operational environment, within which the system's foundation to the practices helps monitor the progress from leadership to results through measurement, analysis, and knowledge management. The idea here returns us to the first three questions, in how you might know the performance level of your organization. This foundation of measuring for results is the critical link in all arguments related to why change for the sake of improvement is in order. Additionally, within the framework, each component of the system is covered in detail with ideas for application and measurement. Ultimately, Baldrige excellence should be the goal of all organizational leaders, but the kind of rare success bred by it is of the work kind. It is not an assessment you outsource. It is a continuous process of acting,

---

[18] Baldrige Performance Excellence Program. 2015. *2015–2016 Baldrige Excellence Framework: A Systems Approach to Improving Your Organization's Performance (Health Care)*, iii. Gaithersburg, MD: U.S. Department of Commerce, National Institute of Standards and Technology. http://nist.gov/baldrige

evaluating, learning, improving, and repeat, like most of the other tools recommended by the integrative leadership model. Unique to it, however, is that it approaches excellence according to assumptions held alongside strategic leadership practices, and it could easily integrate your full-fledged outputs from anticipatory leadership practices as a means of enhancing its framework while also enhancing your anticipatory processes.

Summary

The adaptive cycle promoted the notion of an engineering problem that every organization needs to solve at least once and often regularly. This problem relates to selecting the proper technologies for the production and distribution of a product or service the organizational leadership has chosen for strategically competing within a particular domain. Essentially, the solution is a systems choice, the development or selection of a system that can implement the strategic will of the organizational leadership. Whether you consider the OCAI and the complementary MSAI and/or the Baldrige Excellence Framework to help in the establishment of your strategic leadership practices, the problem still needs solving. Strategic leadership practices emphasize the industry view of the organization. Unlike anticipatory vision, where all meta-domains are under observation to some degree, strategic vision focuses for greater clarity and alertness within the organization and throughout its competitive industry. Its aim is to make the best possible choices with the resources available, evaluate the quality of those choices over time, and adjust future choices according to the results with the goal to improve. Improvement, in this realm, means an intentional development that affects your organization in a manner that helps it achieve its mission to a greater degree than prior to its implementation. It does not simply mean more. Strategic leadership is the force behind the potential truth: less is more, which can mean an intentionally focused effort will likely lead to better results than a haphazard, do-everything, buckshot activity.

CHAPTER 7

Administrative Leadership: Performing

There can be economy only where there is efficiency.
Benjamin Disraeli | British Prime Minister

All the preparation in the world combined with every strategic tool and decision platform would still be insufficient for extraordinary organizational leadership. To round out the process "administrative leadership" is needed. The reason for the name has to do with the importance of leadership on the spot, in each and every situation. There is a kind of leadership that must be prevalent and yet distinct from the anticipatory and strategic processes, though integrated with them. This kind of situation-based, repetition-strong leadership is akin to management, but it bears a heavy emphasis on people orientation in accomplishing objectives. Essentially, where anticipatory leadership scans the horizon and calculates the odds of success, and strategic leadership sets the course and plans for the worst, administrative leadership sets all hands on deck to keep things running.

It needs to be noted that this kind of leadership is often argued as being management and therefore not leadership. This false dichotomy has long been held, as proponents argue that leaders and managers are supposedly separate classes of supervisors. In the May–June 1977 edition of the *Harvard Business Review*, Abraham Zaleznik took this question to task with the piece, "Managers and Leaders: Are They Different." In a 1992 reprint of the piece, he suggested that,

> A critical difference between managers and leaders lies in the conceptions they hold, deep in their psyches, of chaos and order. Leaders tolerate chaos and lack of structure and are thus prepared to keep answers in suspense, avoiding premature closure on

important issues. Managers seek order and control and are almost compulsively addicted to disposing of problems even before they understand their potential significance.[1]

John Kotter built upon that argument with another article, first published in 1990 and reprinted in 2001, which suggested the differences did not necessitate mutual exclusivity; rather, he argued for their complementarity. Kotter wrote that "Management is about coping with complexity … without good management, complex enterprises tend to become chaotic in ways that threaten their very existence …. Leadership, by contrast, is about coping with change."[2] Management, in this sense, is a mindset and skillset, which leaders need to cultivate for the work transition that occurs between the peaks and troughs of strategic change. Moreover, it is this mindset and skillset, constrained by strategic choices, that is herein called "administrative leadership." The reason for my emphasis on administration should be obvious, that it is this set of leadership practices that oversee and administrate the daily choices of an organization's strategic path. It is leadership, because it is held within the paradigm that change is ongoing and being harnessed through the other leadership practices.

What It Is: The Mindset and Language

Along the lines of the management toolkit, Gary Yukl and Richard Lepsinger note that "operational planning, clarifying roles and objectives, monitoring operations, and solving operational problems" are the key impact behaviors of leaders intending to increase efficiency and reliability within organizations.[3] These are highly indicative of administrative leadership, as its endgame is continuance, and such behaviors are clearly aligned with management activities. The key difference, therefore,

---

[1] Zaleznik, A. 1992. "Managers and Leaders: Are They Different?" *Harvard Business Review* 70, no. 2, p. 131.

[2] Kotter, J.P. 2001. "What Leaders Really Do." *Harvard Business Review* 79, no. 11, p. 86.

[3] Yukl, G., and R. Lepsinger. 2004. *Flexible Leadership: Creating Value by Balancing Multiple Challenges and Choices,* 62. San Francisco: Jossey-Bass.

between pure management and this kind of administrative leadership is the impetus of strategic leadership guiding and guarding the behaviors' application. Thus, my argument is that administrative leadership *would* be simple management without strategic leadership's initiative, meaning strategic leadership can exist without administrative leadership, but not the reverse. The latter takes the leadership process within an organization to a higher level, empowering a synergy of doing "the right thing" and doing that right thing excellently. To be more specific, consider the adaptive cycle and how a solution to the entrepreneurship problem leads to an engineering problem and then to its solution; and in turn, that leads to an administrative problem. Management is the consideration of that administrative problem without the adaptive cycle as context. Administrative leadership, however, is the application of shrewd management with the adaptive cycle in mind. It's management-mindedness supportive of strategic change. The motivation value of administrative leadership, then, is the important role it plays in creating organizational slack by refining the engineering problem's solution, thereby making room for new solutions to new entrepreneurship problems to be discovered.

The administrative leadership mindset aims to stabilize the execution of strategic efforts by reducing the uncertainty that naturally accompanies new activities. Such aligns well with Yukl and Lepsinger's (2004) flexible leadership model, being tasked with ensuring efficiency and reliability. Because their model is built on behaviors that prove leadership's presence, their model assesses this leadership need by a combination of (a) "employee productivity, direct cost of operations, cost of sales, and return on assets," and (b) the, "number of product defects caused during production, errors or omissions in providing products or services, avoidable delays in production or delivery of products or services, customer complaints, and accidents or injuries to employees or customers," where the former category deals with efficiency and the latter with reliability.[4] To prove "leadership" in these categories, leaders will utilize a combination of goal setting programs, quality and process improvement programs,

---

[4] Yukl, G., and R. Lepsinger. 2004. *Flexible Leadership: Creating Value by Balancing Multiple Challenges and Choices,* 12. San Francisco: Jossey-Bass.

cost reduction programs, performance management systems, structural arrangements, and recognition and reward systems.

Some of those categories will be more easily adapted for your health care contexts than others, but the notion of observation for the sake of proving efficiency is nevertheless valuable. It is a form of leadership analytics at work. Every assessment will generate value to the degree that it fits your organization's goal interest. Observation is for the sake of maintaining strategic alignment over the long run. As Yukl and Lepsinger wrote,

> Although each of these approaches can potentially add value and help an organization enhance its performance, the success depends on whether an approach is appropriate for the situation, whether it is implemented effectively, and whether it is supported by leaders at all levels of the organization.[5]

Given the earlier discussion of generic strategies, it should be noted here that administrative leadership of this kind is especially important for their extensive execution. Programs and efforts to decrease waste and rework are akin to decreasing input costs for manufacturing. As the workplace complexity rises, organizations have an increasing need for resource efficiency. It can become tempting to not delineate the work procedures, expectations, and schedules, as one moves closer to the work itself (i.e., as the levels of hierarchy decrease), but that generally leads to disorganization and disunity. The reason for the breakdown in organization management by measures, and the apparent absence of free and flexible decision making, can be found in how hierarchies breed opposition by disconnecting individuals from one another's goals. When we separate units according to their tasks without expressing their mutually reinforcing goal positions, we give each no reason to promote the other's good. We give ourselves no reason to reallocate resources to our hurt and the help of another unit that would ultimately help us more down the road. We narrowly focus on the goal-building objective we have been assigned and not on the organization-unifying goal itself.

---

[5] Ibid, 77.

Administrative leadership responds by keeping the aims of strategic leadership in the forefront, but it breaks those goals into accomplishable chunks according to divisions. It also identifies manageable schedules and accountability for that work. Additionally, replicable processes are necessary for scalability. And since organizations need added flexibility to innovate on processes to increase their efficiency, administrative leadership makes room and plans in vulnerability expectations (taking into account negative effects from any proposed change beforehand). Programs that identify and reduce customer complaints and formerly unaddressed issues improve product development and quality assurance and lead to more motivated employees and better asset returns. Furthermore, reliability gains in procedures ultimately translate to safer work environments and forecasting. When forecasting reliability for the internal situation improves, a major task is completed toward more effective anticipatory leadership (energizing the adaptive cycle). Again, it should not be assumed that the three forms of leadership practices simply follow in step-by-step order. They are all active concurrently and integrate with one another. What has been described in delineating their purposes, however, should help in understanding the key approaches to leadership which initiates innovation, reacts against it, and builds upon it.

Before delving into a couple powerful and proven tools of administrative leadership, we first need to address its other purpose beyond building efficiency and reliability into the execution of strategic decisions. That other purpose becoming ever more important with time is: building additional support systems for entrepreneurial insight development. Remember, this was a point highlighted in Chapter 4 in reference to the administrative problem of the adaptive cycle. Added stability stemming from solutions to the administrative problem help fuel this work by reducing the input resource needs, whether for:

- Personnel because task completion time decreases;
- Material resources because of economies of scale and duplicated procedural processes; and
- Experienced perspective on true needs and waste, or otherwise.

As those systems for efficiency and reliability emerge and improve the execution and reduce the resource demands of strategic decisions, the capacity of the organization should increase in reference to the initial resource allocations. Essentially, this means the system should develop slack. You have people who can check more rooms in less time, more experienced methods of cleaning, or of identifying needs. You might have better operational expertise with your telecommunications systems, proprietary software, or organizational decision making processes. These would allow you to make the same decisions as you have previously made in less time and expend fewer resources in the process. What, then could happen as a result? You may experience one of two happenings.

First, your organization might become tighter and continuously more efficient and reliable. Hopefully, however, you realize that such a choice bears the added concern of locking you into a very inflexible competitive position. It could be a huge winner, but it would demand incredible faith amidst these rapidly changing health care circumstances and market assumptions and great uncertainty within our regulatory environment. Second, your organization could continue to operate more efficiently and reliably without changing its allocation of resources, meaning that while your resource demands go down, you continue to operate under the same needs assumptions. In that scenario, you end up having a lot of leftover materials or time, which functions as a very comfortable buffer in case your circumstances shift dramatically and your needs change on the fly. While such seems to be a wonderfully safe tactic, in fact, this kind of stocking up for emergencies is dangerous, because it does not consider the ramifications of reallocating resources and reevaluating risk. For example, by continuing to save time in certain tasks without reallocating any of it, your personnel are, at best, only improving their competence in their current roles and responsibilities. That improvement is only commensurate with their behaviors, and so their role and responsibility competence will not improve beyond that task list. Neither of these options displays a healthy approach to risk management or opportunity management. Moreover, unwillingness to engage in new solution-crafting (for the complicated rather than complex aspects of the environment) with some of the organization's resource slack is a denial of the adaptive cycle premise that the environment, including the competitive environment, is regularly changing.

This is the often forgotten power and duty of management, which is not forgotten with administrative leadership, that of leveraging the slack resources for reinvestment on entrepreneurial and engineering problems. Your efforts at measuring across the organization for the sake of understanding opportunities for efficiency and then acting on them will also give you an indication of the quality and quantity of resources that are saved in time as you become more efficient. Moreover, discovering efficiency and reliability opportunities in one area will often lead to patterning processes in other areas for scope gains, for example, you institute a rule to cut down on paper waste in one department and see it works without creating obstacles for work and keeps the area cleaner and documents more manageable, then you test it in analogous areas throughout the organization to identify the validity of the rule. With the saved direct and indirect resources, which are known only if information is measured and progress tracked, you are able to duplicate efficiency gains and leverage savings in areas of uncertainty—on those innovation and entrepreneurial problems.

Reinvesting slack for anticipatory and strategic leadership practice gains is critical to why administrative leadership practices need to be thoroughly pursued. The better you are at what you do on a daily basis, the less anxiety those routine activities produce by their protocol and less chance those activities have of slowing your healthcare organization's strategic path. Thus, you have the capacity to build new kinds of systems, not the kind which directly solve the entrepreneurship or engineering problems (if they did, then this would not be a practice of administrative leadership), but rather the kind which support the practices of anticipatory and strategic leadership. Examples of such solutions include monitoring systems for product output and performance evaluation, such as turnover rates, patient satisfaction, lengths of stay, product profitability, R & D expenses, and general budgeting. These investments are indirect supports. If you remember from our discussion on innovation in Chapter 2 how the spectrum of innovation with regard to technology can entail supporting technologies, then you have an idea of what a leadership practice that indirectly supports efforts to solve entrepreneurial and engineering problems looks like. For example, if your strategic planning efforts are fairly nascent or old and stodgy, then improving them would be an administrative leadership effort, since it would indirectly affect the efficiency and reliability of that anticipatory and strategic leadership behavior. You might install new planning software or streamline your booking process for leadership retreat venues, or your HR department could add new personnel to key areas that facilitate the anticipatory and strategic leadership functions. In particular, regarding personnel, areas that focus on customer preferences and the market conditions will prove especially important to increasing your external foresight and organizational communication competencies, the latter of which is at the core of administrative leadership. The dependability of information and the consistency of its flow may even be its essence.

What It Does: The Tools

Quint Studer's Health Care Flywheel

In his personal and powerful work *Hardwiring Excellence,* health care leader Quint Studer provides nine principles of service and operational excellence to help health care organizations achieve bottom-line results. These principles guide actions that Studer argues help create momentum for changing the organizational culture of healthcare environments. Since we have already looked into the general components of organizational cultures, here we are more focused on health care in particular and the kinds of principles and practices that facilitate the efficiency of our efforts and the opportunities they can create. This flywheel Studer promotes consists of three components: self-motivated passion (the initial driver), prescriptive to-do's that the nine principles guide, and the results of the actions across each of five organizational pillars (people, service, finance, quality, growth). Studer argues that this model illustrates the capacity for change within a healthcare organization that can remind its people of their purpose for being in the industry, prove through actions how their work is worthwhile, and ultimately that they are making a difference (as is the organization on the whole).

The first action for turning the flywheel is passion, which Studer speaks about in regard to self-motivation and that organizations need to do more on the end of constraining themselves rather than aiming to add something to their employees. Basically, managers do more to limit the passion their people have, day in and day out, than their people do to lose motivation. Their personal reasons for being involved in health care were already self-motivating. It tends to be operational policy and failing systems that put the hurt on that motivation and passion. We must do what we can, therefore, to remove obstructions and enhance the corporate conversation about success. Perhaps one of Studer's greatest and most obvious points is that in healthcare we are trained to highlight problems so that they can be assessed and executed against. That kind of mindset, however, rarely has a chance to celebrate—a necessary and healthy behavior of sustainably high-achieving organizations. In that light, and as reiterated through Principle Nine, recognizing and rewarding success undergirds the construction of systems administrating and communicating value and achievement. You see, Studer's principles for facilitating outstanding healthcare outcomes function as fantastic guidance for administrative leadership practices.

The second action for turning the flywheel is the set of prescriptive to-do's that he recommends for producing the organization's desired results in the five pillar areas. Measuring those areas tends to revolve around evidence of: (1) lowering turnover, (2) raising satisfaction across stakeholders, (3) improving service and quality, (4) increasing service capacity, and (5) improving the financial status.[6] Results accrue when we follow the prescriptive behaviors for handling organizational problems that inhibit our strategic path and help us adjust course. According to Studer, these prescriptions are guided by Nine Principles. They are:

1. "Commit to excellence."
2. "Measure the important things."
3. "Build a culture around service."
4. "Create and develop leaders."
5. "Focus on employee satisfaction."
6. "Build individual accountability."

---

[6] Studer, Q. 2003. *Hardwiring Excellence,* 50. Gulf Breeze, FL: Fire Starter Publishing.

7. "Align behaviors and goals with values."

8. "Communicate at all levels."

9. "Recognize and reward success."[7]

Each principle underpins particular administrative leadership practices that lead to a high-performance culture. These practices, in turn, produce results that our people can be proud of, which motivates and can help the organization reinforce the sense of purpose intrinsic to our field. As you might imagine, and as intended, this growing sense of purpose contributes to a recycling of the flywheel—refueling employees' passion, reminding them of the value generated through the prescribed activities, and making that value visible in results across the five pillar areas. Let's briefly address the practices each principle promotes.

Principle One deals with the motivation at the heart of all integrative leadership practices. If you are not interested in excellence for the sake of your personnel, your patients, your stakeholders, or even yourself, then you are in the wrong business. The key practices of this principle deal with setting the strategy in a similar format for each unit or division within your organization. The process does not need to be uncreative to be streamlined, and in fact, a clear and bounded process will give people greater freedom to understand where creativity needs to be focused. Moreover, it allows for greater cross-department understanding and interaction, since it establishes mutually reaffirming experiences regarding each's approach to the organization's mission, vision, and values.

Principle Two is where we address measurement as a means to manage the best and most important behaviors we want reproduced across the organization. In essence, this is the principle that motivates us to always think in terms of behaviors, practices, and actions that solve problems, enhance situations with added value, and limit our willingness to let issues fester unaddressed. In their studies, the Studer Group found four common drivers for patient satisfaction, something health care providing organizations need to be intensely concerned with (not mainly for reputation, but for the love of their patients!). These were communication,

---

[7] Ibid., 45–231.

pain management, personal needs, and response to call lights. Thus, the practice of administrative leadership would include the measurement of how well and often and where we communicate with our patients and their receptivity and appreciation or concerns about that communication. It seeks to understand that data with follow-up communication with the patients and put that information gained to use as soon as possible— certainly with the responding patient but also in new circumstances to test for positive feedback. Additionally, the results from measuring all these areas should become open information among the organization. You cannot expect employees to get animated about issues going well or be motivated to higher levels of performance without also giving them the "highlight reels."

Principle Three is about developing a service-oriented culture. The advice given here pertains to two practices. The first has to do with the establishment of teams that gain authority and responsibility for handling matters of process improvement across various issue areas. These are people with personal investment and concern for the area, and they do not simply function as a committee that has ideas; rather, they are vested with the power to implement changes themselves. The second practice deals with keeping people connected to the organization's mission, vision, and values through scripted sayings. These are not pat answers. They are memorized reasons for why you do a certain action a particular way. It keeps patients/clients/stakeholders aware, and it is also a reinforcing mechanism for driving particular behavior. In this way, it affirms the administrative leadership practice of creating systems and promoting behavior that increases reliability. Studer remarks that, "Doctors are the best at Key Words at Key Times....they save a lot of time...they know this will make their patient feel a lot better. So they do it out of both efficiency and concern."[8] There are other practices that also help promote a service-oriented culture, but I will leave you to read the book or contact their Group for advisement on your own.

Principle Four is about creating and developing leaders. And, differently from the book you are now reading, the behaviors Studer

---

[8] Studer, Q. 2003. *Hardwiring Excellence,* 90. Gulf Breeze, FL: Fire Starter Publishing.

highlights are far more administratively oriented. They are streamlining prescriptions (like arrive on time) rather than "ontological prescriptions" (like being generous). For instance, and this is great practical advice in my opinion, he notes, "taking leaders off-site to train them on employee selection, new employee orientation, and retention is crucial."[9] The rule of thumb here is two days off-site for 90 days on-site. Within the vein of developing leaders, he notes that three issues take the lead: ensuring they understand organizational change, how performance moves with personal performance conversations, and the how and why to establish organizational institutes for codifying leadership competencies. Organizational change is the framework in which the latter two issues find their places. It starts with onboarding individuals and moves toward understanding those individuals and ensuring they have proper training and development as gaps are identified. This is followed by leaders emerging (according to their performance behaviors). Simultaneously, those who underperform also emerge. Next, the organization strengthens alignment as low performers exist or are asked to leave because they choose to remain unaligned to the organization's mission, vision, and values through the expected behaviors and the results they generate. In regard to performance conversations, the High-Middle-Low Conversations content offered in this tool is invaluable administrative leadership wisdom.

Principle Five relates to employee satisfaction, and there is one primary activity promoted: rounding for outcomes (health care terminology). This practice entails visiting your different personnel to identify needs, concerns, testimonies of success, and relaying back to them motivating results. The idea here is that people want to see how their work makes a difference, and leaders have a prime opportunity as the face and ears of the organizations they lead to do the most about the bad situations that arise, while hearing the most about the good results accrued. Thus, rounding for outcomes is a practice of keeping your ear to specifics like what equipment is slowing people down, which personnel have done exceptional work that their peers appreciate, with what policies people are disappointed or discouraged, etc., The purpose behind it, of course,

---

[9] Studer, Q. 2003. *Hardwiring Excellence,* 109. Gulf Breeze, FL: Fire Starter Publishing.

is continual improvement across the organization, across units, across personnel, and across activities. And, rounding for outcomes should be measured! The only way to prove development in all areas is taking place is by measuring all areas. If rounding produces desirable behavior that increases efficiency and reliability of the organization's product/service, then keep a tab on its pulse.

Principle Six is about wholesale ownership of the change process and improving performance at every level. If we do not own the mission, then in Studer's terms, we're "renters."[10] One thing to note here is that the administrative leadership practices that these principles encourage are part of the systemic operations of the organization. They are not linearly advanced from one principle to the next. They are altogether promoting high quality habits that lead to outstanding healthcare outcomes. For example, with the effort to instill personal accountability, practices include methods to motivate loyalty and attachment to the organization by giving personnel reasons to own the organization's mission and performance. Much of this is accomplished through giving individuals opportunities to make significant decisions, to voice their guidance and opinions in appropriate settings, and to be rewarded for their attentiveness and contributions to improvements. One additional administrative leadership practice noted has to do with peer interviews, as this helps teams congeal and select people with the competencies the team knows it can benefit from.

Principle Seven is about bringing behaviors into alignment with your organization's goals and values. Studer exclaims, "If there are only a few things you do as a result of reading this book, let one be the adoption of an objective, measurable leader evaluation tool. Then hold leaders accountable for those results."[11] As mentioned previously about the principles' systemic effect, you will notice how this practice highlights accountability as well. In summary of this practice, let me say that it involves the evaluation of how well a leader performs across key pillar areas according to his

---

[10] Studer, Q. 2003. *Hardwiring Excellence,* 167. Gulf Breeze, FL: Fire Starter Publishing.

[11] Studer, Q. 2003. *Hardwiring Excellence,* 189. Gulf Breeze, FL: Fire Starter Publishing.

or her preset goals and results. To ensure this practice takes root, additionally supportive practices like progress reports and implementation plans are recommended. Moreover, other evaluations are also encouraged, specifically for support services. Support services as a whole function analogously to how administrative leadership integrates with anticipatory and strategic leadership. If the latter were the doctors diagnosing and treating patients with the nurse team's support, then support services would be the effort to keep everything else running smoothly so that patients, like organizational goals, can be addressed properly and with the utmost attention and effectiveness.

Principle Eight relates to communication reaching all levels of the organization. It entails putting those you lead in a good position to understand your mission and objectives, and gives them a reason to be loyal and supportive. As an administrative leadership practice, managing up is a fantastic tool for disseminating important information, such as when things are going well and people are not interpreting your sharing as passing the buck or judgment. Writing thank you notes is a key practice of such leadership, as it expresses gratitude for organizationally aligned behaviors and helps generate synergy. Furthermore, you can also put clients/patients/stakeholders in a good position to appreciate your organization by communicating to them in the fashion they most understand: that of feeling informed and in-the-loop about your skillset and experience. In this way, communication is an administrative leadership practice that keeps you and the rest of the organization aware of how success is accruing across units and organizational goals. Studer recommends holding quarterly employee forums and constructing unit communication boards for such communication.

Principle Nine, as previously mentioned, is about recognizing and rewarding success. Practicing this behavior through thank you notes and awards and celebratory events, alongside monetary gain, is a key method of encouraging excellence in performance. Perhaps the most important lesson here for practicing administrative leadership in support of other leadership actions is that you recognize and reward until the particular high-performance behavior is ingrained. With new people entering your organization regularly, you will need to reward them commensurate with their experience and performance history. At the same time, the pursuit of high-performance and outstanding health care outcomes must not stagnate. As times change and your organization is adapting, you will need to creatively construct new ways to reward the innovative behaviors that will keep your organization improving and sustainably competitive. You will want to measure it to manage it, and celebratory motivation will encourage it, not simply for tangible rewards, but also because it recognizes peers who are exhibiting the kind of behavior that displays the purpose of their work and how it makes a difference.

That all being said, I barely scratched the surface of Studer's fantastic approach to an excellent performance culture among health care organizations. His flywheel, pillars, and principles are fantastic aids for the administrative leadership focus that drives the daily behaviors leading to organizational success through ongoing improvement efforts. There are other good consulting formulas and models for health care leadership of this kind, but I have rarely come across one so powerful, personal, and practical as this. Do yourself a favor a pick it up, digest it, and start implementing it in support of your integrative leadership model.

The Memory Jogger™ II: Health Care Edition

When it comes to continuous improvement and effective planning, there are few better reference tools than The Memory Jogger™ guides. Since there happens to be a "Healthcare Edition," I would be remiss to skip its endorsement here.[12] While like with the other tools, there is far too much quality content to cover it fully, we can briefly consider the primary benefits of the Memory Jogger™ II for administrative leadership. Essentially, it offers you several different tools in one spiral-bound book for evidence-based improvement when working with ideas, with numbers, and in teams. These tools are measurement and data-based, looking at actual behavior within the organization, and so they would certainly fit into the administrative leadership paradigm of pursuing efficiency and effectiveness together. Moreover, these tools are based on principles similar to Studer's, that sustainable quality improvement focuses on customers/

---

[12] 2008. *The Memory Jogger II: Healthcare Edition.* Salem, NH: GOAL/QPC.

patients/stakeholders, analyzes the improvements of the entire organization rather than only select areas, involves all personnel in the processes, and combines the data with team knowledge to improve decision making. This edition offers health care organizations over twenty tools for improvement activities, from structured and unstructured brainstorming sessions and cause and effect fishbone diagram drawing to prioritization matrix making and radar chart construction. Though I refer you to the pocket guides, you can also contact the nonprofit organization behind the tool, GOAL/QPC, and request training in the tools' use for your leaders and staff.

Consider the Pareto Chart tool, which is highlighted for its ability to help organizations focus on their key problems.[13] Administrative leadership keeps focused on what the strategy development and execution work has set forth and builds in systems that empower efficient and reliable deployment of organizational activities. The tool is based on the Pareto Principle that 20 percent of sources (inputs) cause 80 percent of any problem (outputs), and it calls for the use of a brainstorming session with existing organizational data to identify possible causes of a problem, with the goal of isolating the "20 percent issue(s)." In the guide, the example issue is, "Why are there delays in processing patients through the Emergency Department; what problems are people having," and so brainstorming looks at previously measured reports from the Emergency Department. After brainstorming, the next step is choosing a measurement unit for comparing data, like frequency. Then, a time period for the study is chosen, during which the frequency of issues can be compared across the brainstormed issues list. After the comparison and documenting the results with tables and graphs (visually plotting the numbers and percentages), the team jointly interprets the findings to answer which issue has the greatest negative impact on your organization. Importantly, the issues that are brought to light may not be equally important, and so the unit you measure across may veil this a bit, which is another reason to use multiple tools to get an accurate grasp of the impact of different issues

---

[13] 2008. *The Memory Jogger II: Healthcare Edition,* 95. Salem, NH: GOAL/QPC.

on your organization's most important goals. Administrative leadership practices like these can definitely help in that respect.

Another tool the reference guide looks at is the Interrelationship Digraph (ID), which helps you search and discover drivers and outcomes, the causes and effects related to solutions you need to implement in particular areas of the organization.[14] For instance, suppose you set your strategic direction, but then in the administration of that aim you are unsure of what kind of localized application will give you the best results. The ID will help you with that by encouraging lateral rather than linear thinking. The steps in ID start with generating a unifying agreement about the primary issue being looked at. Essentially, it starts with defining the problem in order to have a unifying goal: solving that problem. Notice, solutions to problems are a vital component to administrative leadership. In contrast, because anticipatory and strategic leadership focus on complex environments where solution-finding can be a dangerous approach, intentionally or unintentionally circumscribing your alertness to a single path, it has not been unrestrictedly encouraged. With administrative leadership, however, you need focus to gain efficiency, and these tools from Memory Jogger™ will help you achieve it.

After defining the problem, you ensure you have issue experts on your team to give the necessary, credible input for arranging the issues and determining plausible correlations between them and the problem under review. Through team discussion, you seek to determine the priority of relationships and influence and determine which issues are greater influences within a relationship. For instance, does one area (A) exert influence through multiple channels on another area (B), whereas (B) only exerts a single, less significant influence on (A)? The team will go through these kinds of discussions until they have a clear first-round review of the influences among the issues, and then they will rank them according to the influence they exert on the others. After a review and another round of influence strength evaluation, the team will diagram out their final ID, in which the reason/issues are drawn in relation to one another with arrows indicating their dominant influence. The outcome of this

---

[14] 2008. *The Memory Jogger II: Healthcare Edition,* 76. Salem, NH: GOAL/QPC.

tool is a visualization (along with the data that helped the team create it) of what factors are driving influences on others within the organization. As I have asserted multiple times throughout the book, strategic thinking is in many ways systemic thinking. This kind of tool helps you understand the systemic influences on behaviors present in your organization. If you can understand which issues and behaviors are dominant among the fold, then you will have a better grasp on what behavioral changes will actually make a difference in the organization's operations.

Summary

In summary, administrative leadership is about greasing the wheels. Its practices are the kind keeping the organization running in the right direction by supporting the effective decisions strategic leadership practices produced. Since we recognize the environments around us are changing, we have to be agile enough to change with them, which is always a matter of degree when practiced in the momentary actions of day-to-day work. Administrative leadership practices, therefore, are those which execute and support organizational change on the *particular* level. They are the practices that find the shortest path to goal completion and help set the agenda for executing the solutions to engineering problems on a large scale. The tools identified in the chapter point to the need for organizing principles that can help establish mission-oriented activities. Such principles can help us make quicker decisions as to what is good and what could be harmful for our organization. For instance, a principle of setting excellent quality or innovation as the most important aim for personnel and then coupling that with a goal to serve patients' needs all the time would help personnel know how to act or not act in particular situations. They would know their actions should support the delivery of excellent care and that being innovative to do so is looked upon favorably. Different principles may inform personnel otherwise.

Being consistent helps improve the administrative leadership aim of efficient and reliable operations throughout the organization, which leads to improved delivery of outstanding outcomes to all stakeholders. At the same time, the smaller moves helped along by creative measurement and team-based decision making tools support anticipatory leadership practices, offering up the means to introduce evidence-based findings and analysis into the entrepreneurial problem-solving cycle. That all being said, administrative leadership is the most often utilized practice of the integrative leadership model, because it is routinely given opportunity to function. This reality makes it all the more necessary for administrative leadership practices to support the other two components of integrative leadership, since they are no less important. Moreover, through their integration, anticipatory and strategic leadership gains a powerful support when administrative leadership functions streamline the path to outstanding health care outcomes. Of course, there will always be the tension to focus on solutions within administrative leadership practices that must be held at bay when the other two components need to be utilized. Organization's assumptions need to be held loosely in anticipatory leadership, and only through study and analysis and group decision making become more readily accepted in strategic leadership. Ultimately, after refinement, they will become usable in administrative leadership in such a way that they further rather than falter your organization's mission.

CHAPTER 8

An Actionable Framework for the Integrative Leadership Model

In this chapter, I hope to give you a glimpse at what a small health care organization employing the integrative leadership model's practices on a routine basis might look like. The variety of organizations present in the health care ecosystem is great, and each is vastly different in makeup and mission. Thus, this chapter will not be all things to all leaders, but it will give you a picture of application. It will illustrate how implementation is possible, and it just might inspire you or give you the spark of insight necessary to start implementation within your organization. The integrative leadership model is far more robust than most, and so application follows suit in being more pervasive than other models. In a sense, that is what this model always expected and always intended: organizational life is complex and offers more points for improvement and innovation than you can imagine. Thus, no innovative path will be equal to another, though they often share common principles. Parallel lines of thinking lead to innovation, and the leaders that drive them—though being as different as the stars in the sky—have often shared similar assumptions and reasons for their call to change. For our industry, the call for innovation has to do with the radically shifting technological, economic, and regulatory environments.

Our national demographics are changing, and the system that was once a driver of U.S. excellence and pride is quickly becoming the albatross that weighs us down and marks us as backward, lethargic, close-minded, and worse. Certainly, we do a lot of good. We are changing people's lives for the better on a daily basis in powerful ways. We are saving lives and birthing new ones. No one doubts this. But, we are not always doing it as well as modern developments could allow for. This is why we need to create the atmosphere for innovation across the industry; and, as leaders of health care organizations, we have the responsibility to ensure that change happens by setting the standard with our own organizations. To do so, we need to get wise to innovation, which this book has helped with. Next, we need to understand the leadership practices that make innovation a sustainable reality for our organizations, which the preceding chapters illustrated through the integrative leadership model, its constituent parts, and a couple available tools for each that can help you understand the intentions and applications of the practices. What follows is a fictional narrative to help you imaginatively perceive these applications in the field.

The Integrative Leadership of Smiley Heart Healthcare

In June, Giles Knight, the CEO of Smiley Heart Healthcare, came across a report decrying the lack of change in the health care industry amidst a world that was leaving it behind. Suffering was promised for the millions that rely on health care organizations for their general welfare, their do-gooding, their employment, and more, if such organizations do not evolve by means of available innovations and innovative processes. From his decades of experience in both health care and financial markets, Giles agreed almost unanimously about the state of affairs. What bothered him, though, was that similar reports and articles illustrating all the changes going on rarely gave him practical advice he could use. They stirred up emotions and enthusiasm, but they lacked the substance he needed to feel satisfied that change was possible and could happen to the degree desired. The authors rarely said "do this" or "change that" with much specificity, because, as he knew, they were speaking to vast audiences and not just his organization. In the past, when facing crises or issues too big for his experience or expertise to fix or manage, he had brought in some friends who happened to be consulting experts for the health care field along with a couple other industries. Generally, they offered good counsel and plans that were substantial enough for him to get the organization back on track or to make a strategic change, setting the firm up for a stable ride during the next few years. Still, he never felt that he could imitate their process, and in one way, that was the kind of solution he really wanted.

Giles felt there was a need to train his own people in the same ways of thinking that led the consultants to identify problems and solutions. The doctors, staff, and support at the Smiley Heart Healthcare organization were good people, people who cared deeply about their patients and one another. Giles knew they would go the extra mile and had witnessed it often. He wondered, though, that with their proximity to patients and difficult problems on a regular basis, how they had missed identifying the systemic issues his friends in consulting had seen with less proximity and experience with the problems. From his self-development regimen and MBA background, he figured it had something to do with the kinds of questions the two groups asked themselves about what was being experienced and how reflections about those experiences did or did not result in adjustments. Giles thought it might relate to quality improvement, but he was puzzled, for most of the clinicians were highly rated in their fields, and the staff were well-educated and credentialed too. Moreover, they had years of experience and had witnessed many ebbs and flows in the industry. If anything, he thought, they should have caught sight more quickly of some issues that had emerged in recent years and acted with greater energy.

Thinking that another perspective would be helpful, Giles called in Cathy and Mathias, the organization's COO and CFO to help him brainstorm on the topic. Over the past year, they had developed a monthly habit of gathering some metric reports from the leaders they were each developing. Basically, each of them committed to mentoring several top performers across the organization. The idea was not so much to train a replacement or prepare for some immediate succession in case of some personal issue—though they knew it offered that contingency—but to make sure they had people within the organization that were not only reliable but also capable advisors. In one way, these emerging leaders were being developed in the sense of gaining organizational authority and say. Giles knew that having a broader team of cross-functional, multi-level oversight could garner Smiley Heart Healthcare broader and deeper insights for ongoing improvement and community outcomes. Of course, he recognized the responsibility to form and manage that broader team would cost he, Cathy, and Mathias (and the performers they worked with) valuable time and opportunities. Yet, the three agreed it would reap them a more resilient organization down the road. Thus, during the brainstorming session, the C-suite each laid out their mentees' reports by issue and functional area for consideration.

Also during the past year, Cathy had heard from a friend who taught finance at her alma mater that global currencies were changing. As Cathy spoke with her friend, she found out about the field of foresight and the notion of reperceiving your environment in order to test current strategies for weaknesses in the case of dramatic environmental changes (specifically, the business environment). She and Giles got together to consider hosting an on-sight workshop with a handful of the most well-respected clinicians and staff members, where the three along with the others would learn some of the theory and a couple simpler applications of foresight to their own strategic management processes. With scheduling and agreement, they were able to hold the first two of four workshops planned over a two-year period with fifteen individuals. The commitment from the participants was to attend the trainings and to serve in one foresight related capacity for Healthy Heart during the next two years. They already have a lot going on in the organization, and so they decided from the get-go to only craft a few opportunities for foresight work during their infancy with the practice. Furthermore, they had seen far too many organizations learn a tool, expect too much with too little investment of time, training, opportunities for application, and money, and they were intent on not letting that happen. The three C-suiters, therefore, decided to split the fifteen participants into two teams that would get together offsite four times a year (including the two training workshops for follow-up and further development with the foresight training group) to practice their tools. They decided to run this offsite work immediately prior to their strategic development and planning retreat, so that any necessary follow-up would be fresh.

To start, the teams learned the notion of what foresight is and how it can help their organization. As health care professionals, they were notably excited about training and the opportunity to develop such a radical competency. Already big proponents of education, the physicians' interest definitely helped strengthen the flame of intense participation, and splitting the large group into two teams helped instill a bit of friendly competition into the practices. Giles's intention was to have the two groups assume the role of competing consulting firms trying to secure Healthy Heart's contract for strategy advisement. The team whose foresight outputs from each offsite gathering contributed the most would receive a special pin to wear until the next offsite and also be recognized at the quarterly, all-hands-on-deck gathering. To keep the competition from hurting morale elsewhere, the teams were mixed up during each offsite, but the fifteen participants remained the same. Cathy suggested that continuity would be important for the group to have all the trainings before expanding the option to others within the organization. She knew it would keep interest higher within the "first" group, and that it would also allow them to become Healthy Heart's experts of foresight over the long run. Together with Giles, she was intending to develop their own internal training center, and thought foresight would be a good subject for rising leaders. Other areas that would also receive focus would be quality improvement and service excellence.

Giles is not the kind of leader who expects to do every significant action or make every significant decision for the organization. Though very competent, one of his greatest strengths is being able to draw others into the leadership role alongside him. He finds out ways to synergize their competencies with his. Many leaders have to balance the expectation to be the organization's visible expert with the wisdom of knowing that is often an impossible chore. Part of Giles's self-assurance, which helps him feel secure as a leader who does not need to tightly rein in decision making, is the support he receives from the organization's board of directors. Giles has certainly made some great decisions in the past, but he has always demonstrated a high-integrity character that was never unwilling to point out those who helped him reach his and the organization's goals. Of course, he has grown in this capacity to be where he is now, as rarely are leaders confident that this approach will not backfire—and it sometimes does. Yet, Giles takes that chance, and his team of leaders follows his example in that regard. They have a deep trust that builds with each challenge they face together, and each success—and failure—that results. Giles agreed that Cathy's training and learning center was a great idea, and he encouraged Mathias to figure out a way to support the effort financially while he worked with Cathy on the return on investment expectations that the board would be interested in knowing.

"Accountability at every level" is a flag the leaders wave without ceasing. Everyone at Healthy Heart knows the decisions that get made have multiple names and faces attached to them, and that those teams own the consequences from the moment the process or expense or hire is approved. Interestingly, while this seems to bind the leadership, it has seriously freed their followers. Within Healthy Heart, nurses and front desk staff will readily tell you of experiences of how when a plan went awry, even though the consequences accrued to them at the point of contact with patients, leadership came and personally apologized for how the staff member's implementation of the leadership decision was met with unintended harm. The staff member would express how that kind of reinforcement of their doing their job properly and facing the spitfire of negative experiences actually made them feel better about their leadership—as odd as that sounds. It was the meekness of the high-level figures that the apology exposed and made them feel closer and grasp that leaders believed in the staff members and their significance to the organization's reputation and effectiveness in meeting its mission.

Though the foresight trainings are still in process, the leaders noted how participants who were chosen to join from among positions generally considered lower level, which have rarely been involved in past strategic decision making efforts, were often able to provide key, unexpected insights. Mathias judged, based on his grasp of the foresight practice, that it probably had to do with their paradigms about leadership and organizations and the healthcare industry—which were from vastly different vantage points compared to the physicians and administrative leaders. Mathias understood why Cathy's friend had led her to look into foresight, for as a finance professional himself, he had a natural inclination to think about Healthy Heart's future and what kinds of scenarios they might plausibly face. His brief experience with the strategic use of foresight helped him understand that regardless of what they did face, they would be better prepared simply by stress-testing their plans. In that way, their most flimsy assumptions about the future would be revealed. As the primary "money-man" for the organization, understanding how to handle uncertainty is his top priority, and Giles is glad to see Mathias so invested in the process. Additionally, Giles knows that the physicians are partial to Matthias's opinions, because they have had a strong data-based positioning to them. By working with physicians on the foresight exercises, therefore, the physicians on Mathias's teams can observe his financial evaluation processes. Matthias and Giles agreed that this would be a useful exercise for exposing top, cross-functional performers (who rarely interact in such creative environments) to each other's competencies. In fact, the foresight trainers thought it would be a good idea to have Mathias share a bit about how he structures the organization's financial forecasts, and he was tasked with giving a brief presentation on how forecasting relates to foresight. It was an appreciated presentation, and even Giles came to a clearer understanding of their similarities and differences. Moreover, the trainers asked Mathias if he might be interested in polishing the presentation a little more and collaborating on a foresight and forecasting subunit with them. After further discussion with Giles and Cathy, the Healthy Heart leaders determined a strategic partnership in this regard would be better for the organization and Matthias than something separate, as Mathias is too busy to focus on this project alone, and so he would have his mentees and staff work on aspects of the forecasting module as a department project that could also contribute to Cathy's training and learning center effort.

If anyone were to observe the team for long, they would notice that each of the leaders, under Giles guidance, is strengthening his or her ability to prepare for and resiliently address future situations. Simultaneously, they are also growing in their awareness of how their personal investment in the organization is shaping the future they will experience. Though this foresight training experience is the first for each of them, each is intimately aware of how changes external to their organization could dramatically affect their personal and shared futures. Thus, they are quickly grasping the use of the tools they have been taught in the workshop sessions. Primarily, because of its ease of use and rapid results, Cathy has used futures wheels in quarterly meetings with her managers to have them contemplate various issues that could affect their supplies, personnel, and credentialing. After they have been developed, the wheels are used in helping the team think through the plausibility of the potential cause-and-effect relationships. Moreover, each of these quarterly,

"Healthy Tomorrows" meetings, ends with a reflective dialogue on what assumptions the team of operations leaders has with regard to how constrained their future is by particular circumstances and decisions. She has made a serious effort to unlock their leadership potential through the use of the quarterly meeting platform to help them grasp their power to create Healthy Heart Healthcare's future rather than simply acquiesce to what others "decide" for it.

The trio knows each of them expresses particular strengths despite their well-rounded competence. For instance, Giles, by nature of his position and experience is both skilled and expected to be visionary and strategic. From his past education, during the early days of strategy consulting's boom, he learned how models and framing situations could prove useful in analyzing competitive situations. His visionary nature had much to do with his personal interest in positive expectations for the future. As a high achiever, he was more focused on creating exciting and high performing organizations than he was fearful of failing or of lacking the resources he might need to complete a goal. One might say his mindset flowed from this visionary attribute. He envisioned, then strategized, and finally executed. His execution was generally effective, though it was rarely flawless. In a sense, his success came from the combination of powerful analytical capabilities alongside his participatory visioning. Strangely for some, he is not that charismatic of a leader. Maybe when he was a bit younger he might have been considered such a leader, but several years ago he came to view certain charismatic characteristics as potentially detrimental to the participatory culture he wanted Healthy Heart Healthcare to express. Thus, he models some positive attributes that leaders within the organization need to cultivate and some which parallel the charismatic type; but, the leadership trio is a kind of model he emphasizes in order to convince the organization that leaders are chief contributors. The trio does not believe cultivating decision and discussion dominators would help push forward the innovation agenda, which assumes value can emerge across the organization at the point of closest contact. They believe every individual has the capacity to support and advance the quality improvement efforts necessary to keep Healthy Heart at the top of its industry as a bellwether for excellent services and care while also being competitive for payers.

While Giles has much positional authority and is legally responsible for many final decisions, in other matters, regulations establish legal responsibility with his physician counterparts. Because of their trust in Giles and appreciation for his humble and participatory leadership, however, they rarely question his plans. Moreover, they have grown accustomed to his seeking their input, and are thankful for how he reshaped their working environment in such a way that they do not feel competitive with one another; instead, the physicians have been able to overcome their own leadership insecurities by Giles modeling the way, expressing leadership vulnerabilities and seeking advice appropriately. As a whole, the physicians are much more unified as a result, supporting each other's professional development and personal lives in ways even Giles did not expect. The rest of the organization has taken its cue from this transformation.

While Cathy and Mathias are also visionary within their respective fields, their focus on operations and finance has narrowed their paradigms in ways which are helpful rather than harmful. If their roles were reversed with Giles, then it would be a much riskier situation, but having a narrower oversight means they can build expertise and perspective that Giles cannot. This is one reason Giles has been so intent on considering their input as equal to his own. Each of them, like Giles, has some advanced education or credentialing that qualified them to take their respective positions. In both their cases, they have a sense of the necessary tasks that will lead to sustainable improvements in their areas of oversight. This confidence stems in part from work they conducted several years prior, when, at the time, Giles had used some of the budgeted leadership development funds to have the trio read through materials related to the Baldrige Excellence Framework before their annual strategic planning week. When they came together, they realized there was a need to change how they approached strategic planning altogether. Though systems thinking was not a foreign concept to Giles and Cathy, it was wonderfully refreshing—especially for Mathias. In fact, his enthusiasm helped them rethink the whole notion of outcomes within Healthy Heart. With the support of the physician and administrative leaders they directed, they embarked on year-long effort to establish the performance-aimed processes the approach calls for. They had some hits and some misses, but they were fortunate enough that the evidence-based reviews established a sense of fairness everyone appreciated. Furthermore, the effort—though time-consuming and rigorous—helped everyone in the organization learn the impact of their own work on the other divisions. In one sense, it captured the diagnostics of Healthy Heart and gave leadership an important readout in review of how individual behaviors affected overall performance.

These readouts were created by Cathy's team who has a bit more experience with continuous quality improvement than either Giles or Mathias. As the COO, she felt it was her responsibility to ensure the implementation of the Baldrige ideas and suggestions would be standardized, easy to understand and apply, and could offer useful feedback. She got her team copies of the Memory Jogger™ materials, and had them each work on separate tool developments for their respective areas of management at Healthy Heart. The agreement was that she, Giles, and Mathias would give 10 percent of the staff's work week to tool development and review, essentially settling for Friday afternoons, which meant that scheduled tool development time would occur on the heels of the all-hand-on-deck meetings. The trio felt this occurrence would help the tool developers keep the organization's mission and primary goals in view as the tools were constructed. In the end, after four to six months of development (depending on the tool and department), the tools had finished being tested and were rolling out to personnel for use. This was not a surprise for the workers, as many of them had been involved in answering tool-makers' questions through emails and lunch-time interviews, to ensure the tools' usefulness. Thus, after a three-month review, it was determined by the trio that a majority of the tools were helpful for Healthy Heart's organizational improvement—in ways that the Baldrige Excellence Framework would approve and that gave the departments clear pictures of how they were performing in key areas. The less-useful tools were discontinued or revised at Cathy and the department leader's discretion. Most of them determined to revise their tool according to helpful feedback, including a review of what made the successful tools so useful and helpful. Ultimately, it was determined that the team of operations leaders would work to integrate similar tools into a digital platform with a unified display, readily accessible through a mobile device. The IT director confirmed that this was possible to post on their Intranet for easy access and would help as a clearinghouse for all the reports.

As the leadership team prepares for the third foresight workshop, Giles is confident that these measurement and progress-checking tools developed several years ago will continue to be useful and help Healthy Heart stand at the forefront of its region in care and resource stewardship. In tandem, Mathias applauds their investment in such tools. Originally, he was hesitant to invest in training and especially offsite time because the return on investment was murky. Only after learning about the Baldrige competition and follow-up statistics pertaining to those who had engaged the excellence process, was he more at ease. Today, he is one of the organization's biggest cheerleaders for continuous quality improvement and the tools Cathy and her team generates. They have helped provide *his* team with better data for financial forecasting and enabled him to take advantage of the reduced uncertainty the information brings. Given this advantage, he assertively commits more funds to innovation efforts. In one respect, the development and implementation of the tools and systems approach to leading and managing Healthy Heart Healthcare was innovative. It was a shift in the "business model" and led to a sustainable competitive advantage over the years through increased patient and physician satisfaction.

Thinking about how Healthy Heart Healthcare has developed over the past decade, Giles can smirk when reading such fear-mongering articles about rapid change and the future of his industry. He is neither arrogant to think the article is completely untruthful nor is he uninitiated into the difficult work of defining how to act amidst uncertainty. However, he sees the article's failure as one of failing to guide and inspire. Giles's experience has shown him the trouble foggy futures can pose—and the anxiety that burdens leaders who are left without the means to address them. He is clear that his situation would not be much different from the anxious, concerned leader's, were it not for his participatory C-suite developing alongside him, contributing to the vision he seeded, and executing their strategy with dogged optimism. Giles even thinks providence has had a role, though some attribute it to his humility to take his subordinates' perspectives seriously. Giles thinks it would have been ridiculous not to. Remembering an inspirational word about the indispensability of parts of the body to the whole, he thinks: Like with a healthy body, you need healthy systems to survive. Even as a top leader I am, at most, the systems' override. Without the rest, however, we cannot even breathe.

Summary: It's What You Do With What You Know

The story of Giles Knight and his team at Healthy Heart Healthcare illustrates the greater importance of *practicing* leadership when compared to the innocuous nature of positional labels. As with our exploration of the Intel leadership team at the beginning of this book, there is fascinating synergistic effect that takes hold when the combination of strategic management and diverse temporal foci can be exercised among an organization's top decision makers. Simultaneous attention placed on the organization's past, present, and future is impossible unless the vision is shared. This forces us, once again, to notice the differences of a mindset that drives an improvement culture. Among the assumptions that must be changed in order to recognize and reap the benefits of continuous change processes, which are usually aligned with systems thinking, Peggy Holman identifies a kind of old and new way of thinking about quality improvement. As it regards an organization, does management "own" or is "ownership shared?" Regarding information, is it automatically restricted or transparently offered? And, should one operate only within their role or seek opportunities to offer support and expertise? Finally, is goal completion or growth our true aim?[1] The latter inquiries illustrate the new way forward.

Healthy Heart Healthcare is no different from our organizations in its need for flexible assumptions to sustainably drive our changing behaviors. Without the eyes to see, we will not be able to reach the futures we want. Additionally, we will be incapable of preparing for those we do not want. To be fair, sometimes, our organizations need to jump start the process with behavioral change, as actions can speak louder than words—especially when outstanding health care outcomes are the object in view.

---

[1] Jick, T.D., and M.A. Peirperl. 2003. *Managing Change: Cases and Concepts,* 514, 2nd ed. New York: McGraw-Hill/Irwin.

CHAPTER 9

Epilogue

If you are not training and developing the leaders' skill set, they can't succeed. I don't believe that an organization can truly succeed at living its values (e.g., integrity, respect, teamwork, quality) without investing in developing the necessary leadership competencies. If organizations believe it's important to provide employees with the tools to be successful at their jobs, the tools they should provide to leaders are leadership competencies.

—Quint Studer, Hardwiring Excellence, p. 110

In their acclaimed July 2003 *Harvard Business Review* article, "What Really Works," professors Nitin Nohria and William Joyce and business expert Bruce Roberson reveal a powerful insight from their groundbreaking management research: Superior organizational results stem from excelling in four primary management practices alongside *any* combination of two others from a second four essential practices. The four primary management practices that must exist are strategy, execution, culture, and structure. The secondary areas, from which you are to focus on *only* two, are talent, innovation, leadership, and mergers and partnerships. Again, you have to *excel* in these areas. Within the integrative leadership model presented, leadership and innovation can be considered the chosen secondary practices. Parsing them out, strategy and execution are obviously presented, and culture is discussed seriously within the bounds of strategic leadership and the OCAI and MSAI tools and the healthcare culture-focused work of Quint Studer's Nine Principles of service and operational excellence. Structure is also a strong focus of the integrative leadership model, but it shows up less conspicuously—in administrative leadership practices that cut out arbitrary hierarchy and within the discussion of Robert Keidel's triadic model emphasizing the need for cooperative, hierarchical, and autonomous structuring. The integrative leadership model, then, provides leaders with a framework that *really works*.

Thus, it should be clear by this point that integration is *ongoing* for powerful systems of leadership and organizational performance. As continuing research probes, challenges, expands, and extends our strategic management understanding with new and reshaped insights, we can hold some confidence that it will not force us to completely discard everything we have gained—just as the importance of understanding effectiveness never should have pushed us to discard the value of efficiency. Certainly, the foresight practice that I hope you have come to appreciate may give us pause when considering whether our reality could be utterly upended. Either way, however, you can keep expanding your paradigms to alert you to changes your organization would have been blind to otherwise.

For those who may begin this journey from the end (and there is no shame in that, I read conclusions first myself), let me summarize the three leadership practice categories that make up the proposed integrative leadership model like this: Anticipatory leadership practices activate and employ the alerting function of leadership, taking pause prior to decision making to gather, compile, consider, and synthesize conjectures, while also contemplate alternative assumptions about the organization's environment; Strategic leadership practices employ the output of anticipatory leadership practices for analysis and decision making, which includes strategic planning activities; Administrative leadership runs the operations with a mind toward continuous improvement in order to create space for further investment in anticipatory and strategic leadership practices but at reduced costs. To limit confusion about the difference between the practices of anticipatory and strategic leadership, it is also important to reemphasize the roles of strategic management's three activities. Strategic thinking is the work of recognizing opportunities and qualifying possibilities, strategy development is the work of condensing the former step's output into set of integrated targets, and strategic planning is the work of setting up the firing instrument for striking the target given the available resource constraints. The first of the three makes its presence known in each of the three integrative leadership model components, though the second and third remain confined to your strategic leadership efforts. As mentioned at the end of the beginning, it bears repeating now at the end's end: a leadership portfolio of this sort engages a whole innovation cycle from conception through production and into renewal. *This is integrative leadership the execution of a cohesive portfolio of leadership practices that promote outstanding health care outcomes.* As a portfolio, leadership is no longer locked into one diagnostic for organizational health and remedy; rather, leaders have at least three *concurrently* operating diagnostics in the form of the leadership practices and the assumptions undergirding the long-term, medium-term, and present. We gain flexibility with this approach to leadership because the competing needs of present efficiencies, medium-term choices, and long-term contingencies are balanced.

Of all that has been said, I especially hope you have the mind to advance healthcare with innovative efforts and outstanding, performance-oriented leadership. Reading books about leadership will always be easier than engaging in the work of leadership, and so I first commend you for taking the time to continue your self-development and appreciate you for bringing these ideas into your realm of authority. Health care needs interested and competent leadership. Second, I charge you to not let this reading be the culmination of your development. Faithful application is perhaps the best demonstration of comprehension and best way for your organization to benefit from your development. Third, remember that this model is not the end-all be-all of leadership models. It is integrative, and so you should identify ways to adapt its counsel for your organization's unique expression and constraints. The future of healthcare depends on you. Whether it will be outstanding or lackluster is decided at the point of care, and that care depends on the decision making calculus of numerous leaders driving the resourcing of and investment in the industry's innovation. With an eye to the future like Giles Knight might have, ask yourself, can you afford carelessness?

About the Author

A passionate strategist, educator, and advisor, **Dr. David Stehlik** is the Business Administration Program Director for the Keith Busse School of Business and Entrepreneurial Leadership at the University of Saint Francis and the founder of *Fourscene*, a strategy and business education consultancy.

David's leadership experience spans levels and geographies for academia, nonprofits, and health care. He earned a BA from Hillsdale College and his MHA and MBA from the University of Saint Francis. His doctorate from Regent University focused on strategic foresight. He has consulted for the national leaders of organizations in Bulgaria, Macedonia, Romania, Albania, and Serbia as well as U.S. businesses and nonprofits. He is a certified instructor in Continuous Innovation Framework and an active member of the Association of Professional Futurists (APF).

Index

of Smiley Heart Healthcare,
136–145
strategic choice, 67–69
Intel, xvi–xvii, xxxi–xxxiii
intended measurability, 58–60
Internet, xxvi, 13
Interrelationship Digraph (ID), 131
Isaacson, W., xxxii

Johns Hopkins, 29
Johnson & Johnson, 24

Kauffman, V., 10
Keidel's triadic model, 73–79
Knight, G., 136
Kotter, J., 116
Kouzes, J.M., 65

Lampel, J., 105
LASIK surgery, 27
leadership. *See also* integrative
leadership; organizational
leadership
administrative, 67
anticipatory, xxx, 2, 66–67
control. *see* control
defined, 63
efficacy of, 72–73
forms of, 63–64
importance of practicing, 146
and innovation kiss, 63–67
integrative model, 67
organizational, 14. *see also*
organizational leadership
portfolio of, xv–xvi
practices, 65–66
practices, application of, xxx
strategic, 67. *see also* strategy
theory of application, 64–65
The Leadership Challenge (Kouzes and
Posner), 65
leadership control, xxiv–xxv
Lepsinger, R., 72, 116
low-cost provider strategy, 106

Management Skills Assessment
Instrument, 109
mapping plausible scenarios, 96

market cultures, 110, 111
market demand, xx
market innovation, xxii
market niche strategy
based on differentiation, 107
based on low costs, 107
market transactions, xix
McDonald's, 24
McKinsey and Company, 30
Medicaid, 2
Medicare, xxviii, 2
Memory Jogger™ II, 129–132
microprocessor, xxxiv, 93
Miles, R., 67
Minnesota Mining and
Manufacturing (3M), 35
Mintzberg, Henry, 60–61, 104
Moore, Gordon, xxxi, xxxii–xxxiv
morbidity, 22
mortality risks, 22

negotiations, xix, 14, 37
nonprice value, 25–26
Noyce, R., xxxi, xxxii–xxxiv

obesity, xxviii
OCAI and MSAI tools, 147
Ocumetrics Bionic Lens, 28
organizational (internal) audit, 31–32
organizational culture, xvi, xxxi, 51,
81, 107–108, 122
organizational leaders, 31–32, 64, 79
on innovation strategies, 32,
106–107, 113
organizational leadership, xxiv–xxv,
xxvi, 14, 73, 76, 114,
115. *See also* strategic
leadership
organizational maturity, xvii,
xxxiii
organizational strategy, 37, 77, 86,
103, 106
organizational structure, 74–75
Organization Culture Assessment
Instrument, 109
organization's mission, vision,
values, and goals (MVVG)
framework, 48

www.ingramcontent.com/pod-product-compliance
Lightning Source LLC
Chambersburg PA
CBHW061308220326
41599CB00026B/4783